LANGUAGE AND THE STUDY
OF LANGUAGES TODAY

LANGUAGE AND THE STUDY
OF LANGUAGES TODAY

by

MARGARET SCHLAUCH

WARSZAWA • PWN—POLISH SCIENTIFIC PUBLISHERS

LONDON •.OXFORD UNIVERSITY PRESS

Oxford University Press
37 Dover Street
London W1

Distributed outside Poland, Bulgaria, the Chinese People's Republic, Czechoslovakia, the German Democratic Republic, Hungary, Rumania, the U.S.S.R.,
and Yugoslavia by the Oxford University Press

Printed in Poland (D.R.P.)

CONTENTS

CHAPTER 1.   HOW LINGUISTIC SCIENCE AROSE

1. Language a Peculiarly Human Achievement   1
2. Naive Interest in Language   3
3. The Slow Development of Scientific Interest in Language   5
4. The Foundations of Modern Linguistic Science   11
5. Further Achievements of Linguistic Science   16

CHAPTER 2.   FAMILIES OF LANGUAGES IN THE WORLD TODAY

1. What is Meant by the Term "Family of Languages"   19
2. The Indo-European Group   23
3. Finno-Ugric and Basque   28
4. Semitic-Hamitic   31
5. Altaic (Ural-Altaic) and Paleo-Siberian   33
6. Sino-Tibetan and Its Neighbours   35
7. African Groups Today   38
8. Amerindian Families   40
9. Some General Problems   42

CHAPTER 3.   WORDS AND WORD FORMATION

1. Free and Bound Elements in Words   45
2. Some Special Problems Related to Bound Forms   49
3. Morphology and what It Means   51
4. Fused Forms and Etymology   56
5. What Is a Word?   59

CHAPTER 4. WORDS AND THEIR MEANINGS: SEMANTICS

1. The Conventional Nature of Linguistic Signs — 67
2. The Societal Environment of Words — 71
3. General Reasons for Change of Meaning — 74
4. Main Types of Semantic Change — 79
5. Some Special Factors of Social Environment — 83

CHAPTER 5. THE SOUNDS OF A LANGUAGE: RECORDING AND TRANSCRIPTION

1. Early Forms of Alphabets — 87
2. Alphabets and Sounds Today — 92
3. Speech as a Continuum — 99
4. General Trends in Sound Patterns — 102
5. Some Types of Sound Change — 107

CHAPTER 6. THE STRUCTURE OF A LANGUAGE

1. Major Units of Utterance: What Is a Sentence? — 113
2. The So-called Parts of Speech and Their Inflexions — 116
3. Describing Parts of Speech — 122
4. Syntax, or the Relation of Sentence Elements — 128
5. Some Stylistic Implications of Linguistic Structure — 133

CHAPTER 7. CONTEMPORARY APPROACHES TO THE PROBLEMS OF LANGUAGE

1. Language and the Theory of Probability — 138
2. Language and Communication Theory — 142
3. Some Contemporary Analyses of Language — 149

CHAPTER 8. CONCLUSION — 160

SUPPLEMENTARY BIBLIOGRAPHICAL NOTES — 167

INDEXES — 171

CHAPTER 1

HOW LINGUISTIC SCIENCE AROSE

1. LANGUAGE A PECULIARLY HUMAN ACHIEVEMENT

Human beings are animals that talk. This is their supreme differential trait that marks them off from other animals and at the same time elevates them (at least we like to think so) above other animals. By making secondary use of certain organs, most of which primarily serve other purposes (lips, teeth, tongue, etc.), people have learned over the course of uncounted ages to develop a number of extremely elaborate, subtle, and at the same time swift and efficient systems of communicating orally with one another. The specific systems vary widely from one part of the world to another, but all of them alike are marked by the same truly amazing ability: they utilize vibrations of air emitted from our mouths in order to convey wishes, instructions, commands, emotional statements and even sets of abstract logical propositions to our listeners' ears, both speedily and on the whole accurately. Relatively recently men have also learned to write, using various types of alphabets: recently, that is, if we take into account the total span of time during which we know that mankind has inhabited the earth before history began. But the writing (or printing, as the case may be) is only a conventional way of representing what is spoken. In other words, the visual appeal is merely a substitute for the auditory. The basic situation is and remains that of one person talking to another and evoking replies.[1]

Or better still, let us say it is the situation of people speaking together in social groups. Such groups may vary in number from a tiny tribe to a huge nation, but the point is that they do constitute

---

[1] For the sake of simplicity I ignore such special situations as communication among deaf-mutes. Here too an elaborate system has been devised as substitute, but it is likewise historically late.

groups that work and play and struggle together, largely with the help of a common language. Even when two individuals are alone, engaged in the most private conversation, their ability to talk thus is conditioned on the joint experiences they have had all their lives in common talking with others, and the way they express themselves will be conditioned by their background of this social experience, no matter how personal and original their communication may seem to them at the time. Moreover, the very substance of what they say will be conditioned by an inheritance of knowledge and attitudes transmitted from one generation to another by the instrumentality of speech.

Language is, then, a fundamental means of preserving, transmitting and continuously enriching the achievements of human culture. Not only is it very delicate in structure, but it is capable of indefinite modification and expansion as society evolves and becomes ever more complex.

Yet the essential mastery of any given language in the human family, with all its implicit complexities and potentialities, is gained by children when they are still extremely young. At first they imitate words and phrases; then they begin to adapt patterns and formulas to wider situations—making "mistakes," of course. (A "mistake" is here understood simply as a deviation from the norm set by adult speakers.) An English-speaking child may first learn to repeat a word like *mama*, and next a phrase like *bread's all gone* or *good-bye daddy*. The phrases will give him a chance to make substitutions like *cake's all gone*, *milk's all gone* or *good-bye mummie*—sometimes indeed what may be called crossed substitutions like *good-bye bread* or *daddy's all gone*. Having heard a grown-up remark of him that he wants a bottle, he will echo the formula and say *wants a bottle* (third person) when referring to himself. But the important thing is that in an astonishingly short time the child masters the basic structure of his language, he corrects the "mistakes" first made because of mechanical imitation and like causes, and has soon learned to fit the "irregular" forms into an otherwise regular pattern (English *I went* instead of **I goed*; Polish *szedłem* instead of—let us say—**idźlem*). What is more, the child gains an ability to create all sorts of new sentences never previously enunciated and also to understand such new sentences when spoken by others. Thanks to his mastery of the overall pattern, he is in possession of an instrument of unlimited potential expansion. He will be able to progress from a simple concrete affirmation like "I see the dog" to an abstract one like "I see the implications of your sophisticated argument." And this ability of his will be shaped and established in the early, pre-adolescent years. After that it will merely be a question of adding to the sum total of words at his disposal, a much less taxing requirement. If he hears an unfamiliar term in an otherwise familiar context, he need only ask the speaker "What do you mean by that?"—or look it up in a dictionary.

What is true of learning one's own language is also true of learning a foreign one. The best years are the early ones, before children have developed reasoning power to a very high degree. They rely on imitation chiefly, not rationalization. Yet language is the vehicle of reasoning, and is itself a highly abstract system of communication. The situation is paradoxical, it would seem. We shall return to it later. For the moment it is enough to point it out.

2. Naive Interest in Language

An outstanding characteristic of languages in general is that people use their own tongues unconsciously. This results naturally from the fact that they learn them young and absorb them in what we have called the prerational age or the age of routine memorizing. As children, they accept their elders' speech habits uncritically. But later on they may notice certain ambiguities and inconsistencies in their native speech, and begin to wonder about them. They will thus begin to pose some questions which are of necessity naive, but represent the beginnings of scientific curiosity. English and French children, for instance, are taught in school a system of orthography that is extremely archaic. In France they must learn to write *beaux*, which looks as if it represented at least five separate sounds (even six, if x is to stand for something like ks) — and yet they know that in talking they enunciate only two sounds (*bo*). Or in England they must learn to write two different words, *knight* and *night*, when they actually pronounce them identically as something like *nait*. Here the spellings reflect an earlier state of the language concerned. Similarly in Polish a distinction is made in spelling between *może* and *morze, tuż* and *tusz*, although in practice those are identical word-pairs. There are historical reasons for such aberrations, but it is the rare student who will wonder about them, since he is early conditioned to accept them. If he does question them, he is already on the track that will lead him to linguistic science.

Such a student, if he pursues the study of other languages besides his own, may find further reasons for questioning and wonder. An English youth learning German cannot fail to be struck by the likeness of word-pairs such as *father*: *Vater*. (Here the German spelling of the initial sound obscures the likeness to a certain extent; in both cases the sound is what is conventionally represented by the letter *f*.) A Polish youth learning Russian cannot fail to be struck by the likeness of word-pairs like *serce*: *cepдцe* or *sierp*: *cepn*. But the deductions drawn from such observations by a naive observer may be quite wrong. He may think that one language must necessarily have borrowed from another when he finds similar forms in both of them. Sometimes to be sure he will be right, for instance when he notices that English *guard* and French *garde* are similar and therefore probably closely related. (They are also related to *ward*, but that is not so obvious.) However, if he thinks that English *care* and Latin *cura* are closely related because they sound somewhat alike, he will be deceeied. He will of course fail to recognize the relationship between many word-pairs actually related, like *cepдцe*: *heart*—but that is still another matter. The main thing is that he begins to look at language inquiringly and even critically instead of accepting it without question, unconsciously, and that is the beginning of wisdom.

Still another factor which may possibly stimulate speculation about one's own language is the existence in it of rare or exotic terms. Sometimes these are misinterpreted, but the very misinterpretation evinces a certain effort to understand and assimilate the unusual words. For instance, English has taken over from the French a word *sirloin* referring to a part of a loin of beef. The first element of the word is a mere prefix meaning upon or above (from Latin *super*, by way of the French). Hence: above the loin (French *logne*). But since the word was originally strange to English, a story was created to explain its existence, based on a misunderstanding of its etymology. According to the story, a feudal prince of England was so delighted with the cut of beef served to him that he decided to knight it and proclaim it "Sir Loin." About this anecdote W. W. Skeat remarks in his *Etymological Dictionary of the English Language*: "The story about turning *loin* into *sir-loin* by knighting is mere trash." True enough. And one could cite many analogous stories, equally unfounded, from other languages. But the fact is that such fictional anecdotes reflect a naive yet laudable desire to explain the origin of terms as yet insufficiently understood in a given language.

From time to time bilingual speakers notice that they cannot find an exact equivalent for the term of one language in another. Thus it will be found difficult to render into English an equivalent of German *gemütlich* or *Angst* or *Weltanschauung*. Such practical difficulties will also call attention to the limitations of any given language in comparison with another, and also arouse interest in the nature of and reason for their differences.

3. The Slow Development of Scientific Interest in Language

The users of the three best-known languages of ancient times— those of India (i.e., speakers and writers of classical Sanskrit), Greece and Rome—subjected their own tongues to orderly investigation, and thus systematic descriptions were achieved. Of the three Sanskrit fared best. Its alphabet was exceptionally well adapted to the recording of the actual sounds of speech without superfluities or ambiguities, and it was arranged according to a valid phonetic system. Moreover, the Indian grammarians (notably Pānini, ca 300 B.C.) worked out a detailed and accurate analysis of the structure of Sanskrit, which arouses admiration to this very day. This fact was primarily due to the zeal in preserving and elucidating the sacred texts of the Vedas. The Greeks, following their philosophical bent, speculated on the possible relationship between an action or a thing and the name given to it, and indulged in some fanciful etymologies of words. (Thus Plato in the dialogue *Cratylus*—or better, *Kratylos*; but the discussion appears to be only partly serious.) Beginning with Plato and Aristotle and continuing with the Stoics, the Greeks also developed grammatical descriptions of their own language recognizing parts of speech, declensions, conjugations, so-called grammatical "rules" (with their "exceptions") and the like. In other words, they too became conscious of their own linguistic structure, but they were quite incurious about those of other peoples. As is well known, they called non-Greeks barbarians, a term of contempt which basically means "those who stammer incomprehensibly." Such an attitude blocked any explorations which might have led to an understanding of the similarities and differences among languages surrounding them.

The Romans followed the Greeks and learned from them. Their grammarians translated or adapted into Latin much of the Greek terminology: the general term case (*casus*), for instance, and the names for the specific cases (nominative, accusative, etc.). They shared the Greek attitude towards "barbarians"—but excluded themselves, naturally, from this undesirable category. Some attention was paid by them to questions of etymology, but it would have been better if they had not done so. Disregarding the division of words into elements which we today roughly designate as root, stem, and endings, they concentrated on partial, accidental similarities in order to guess at relationships. Thus *vulpes* (genitive *vulpis*) was interpreted as "fly-foot," from the verb *volere* meaning to fly, and *pēs* (genitive *pedis*) meaning foot. The difference of vowels in the first roots, *vul-/vol-*, and of consonants in the second, *pēs/ped-* seemed not worth noticing. The Romans even undertook to explain relationships of like-sounding words with opposite meanings on the theory that pure antithesis could engender cognate forms: thus *bellum* "war" was supposed to come from *bellus* "beautiful" precisely because war isn't beautiful. The theory was summarized in the saying *Lucus a non lucendo.* That is, a grove is called *lucus* because it has presumably nothing to do with being lucent or light.

The Middle Ages were no more favourable to an independent, scientific approach to language. Latin continued to be the instrument of communication among scholars in Western Europe for many centuries after the collapse of the Roman Empire. The two Latin grammars of Donatus (ca 400 A.D.) and Priscian (ca 500 A.D.), written in the late Empire, continued to be the basis of instruction. They served a practical purpose but did not stimulate broader curiosity. The promulgation of fantastic etymologies continued, with a high-handed disregard for the presence or absence of equivalent sounds in the words compared. Thus Lactantius (a Church Father of the fourth century) cheerfully informs us that ears were called *aures* from their function of drinking in (*hauriendis*) sounds (the significance of initial *h* in the latter word being quite ignored). The Roman grammarian Varro, a contemporary of Cicero, was actually responsible for some of these wild guesses. They were repeated and amplified by Isidore of Seville (died 639) in the section of his compendious encyclopedia which he devoted to the origin of language. Adam, he tells us, gave names to the beasts in Hebrew. In Latin too their names will be found to be appropriate. The boar *aper* is so called because of his fierceness, or *feritas,* "if we just take away the letter *f* and substitute a *p,*" he remarks naively, not even mentioning the subtraction of the initial *a.* Horses or *equi* are so called from *aequalis* meaning equal, because they are yoked together. And so on.

These early Christian writers were, then, simply continuing a policy of uncontrolled guessing already initiated by their classical predecessors. But a new tendency in medieval thinking was destined to militate still further against a truly scientific study of words and their origins, namely the all-pervading passion to find occasions for moral instruction in the phenomena of nature and culture. For most authors the verification of fact became far less interesting than the quest for spiritual edification. The writings of Rabanus Maurus illustrate the tendency to a marked degree. Even the authors of encyclopedias depended on the technique of compilation rather than original research in scientific matters until the time of Roger Bacon. The plastic arts and literature were to a great extent also permeated with a purely homiletic spirit, inhibiting to first-hand investigation.

Individual names were also exploited to serve the ends of instruction. For instance, Jacobus de Voragine (13th century), author of the *Legenda Aurea* or *Golden Legend*, sometimes began the biography of a saint with an exposition of the supposed hidden significance of his or her name. A single name could have more than one significance. Thus the name of St. Cecilia is first interpreted by Chaucer, following Jacobus, as meaning a lily of heaven, from Latin *coeli lilia*; next as meaning the way for the blind (folk), from Latin *caecis via*, and further to a total of five etymologies which are obviously mutually exclusive. One of them goes back to the principle *Lucus a non lucendo*, already mentioned: Caecilia is so called precisely because she lacked blindness or *caecitas* (*Caecilia quaisi caecitate carens,* said Jacobus; Chaucer paraphrases this as "wanting of blindness").

Examples like this could be multiplied. In fairness to de Voragine and Chaucer and others like them, it should be remarked that they were not really pretending to offer etymologies as we understand the term today. They simply didn't care whether one or the other of the proposed origins was historically correct, so long as it was morally edifying; and they were surely intelligent enough to know that not more than one could accord with the facts. It was merely that the facts of linguistic history were supremely indifferent to them.

Despite the attitudes and preoccupations inimical to scientific study of languages, some observations were made and some questions were raised in the Middle Ages which pointed the way to more fruitful inquiry later. Discrepancies were noted between certain rules of classical Latin grammar and usages of the Vulgate translation of the Bible. Some knowledge of Hebrew and Greek as well as Latin existed in England in the seventh century; the Venerable Bede was able to explain correctly the Greek terminology of ancient rhetoric in the book he wrote (ca 700 A.D.) concerning the figures of speech and tropes to be found in the Vulgate translation of the Bible. A different kind of linguistic skill was employed by the Anglo-Saxon scholar Aelfric when he wrote a grammar of Latin in Old English for his students (ca 1000 A.D.). In the Latin preface he pointed out that this text would help them to understand the grammar of their own tongue. His attitude shows an unusual respect for the vernacular. In the early 13th century the learned Robert Grosseteste, Bishop of Lincoln, studied both Greek and Hebrew in order to equip himself to persuade Jews the more effectively (by peaceful means) of the truth of Christianity.

These sporadic efforts heralded the great upsurge of interest in such problems at the time of the Renaissance. The scholarly edition of the Greek New Testament by Erasmus (in 1516) invited careful comparison with the Vulgate. Thus certain inaccuracies in the latter came to light. Hebrew as well as Greek was now widely studied at universities, and curiosity was extended to the languages previously neglected. At first the results may be said to have been a quantitative rather than a qualitative improvement in the situation. Men knew more facts about more languages than previously, but the principles of their various historical developments were not yet grasped, and there was little insight into their structures. An example of compendious information is the *Mithridates* of the Swiss scholar Gesner (published in 1555), so named from King Mithridates of Pontus (last century B.C.), said to have known twenty-five languages.

Antiquarians, lawyers, ecclesiastics, literary historians and others continued to extend the field of interest in the 17th and 18th centuries. English lawyers, for instance, needed to know Anglo-Norman (a special dialect of Old French), as well as Latin and Old English, if they were to understand the legal documents of the Middle Ages which were still recognized as pertinent. Research in special vocabularies of such disciplines helped to stimulate English

lexicography, which is represented by a whole series of distinguished dictionaries produced in two centuries, the 17th and 18th,
reaching a high point in the famous one by Dr. Samuel Johnson
(1755). A very fruitful field of interest was cultivated in the Scandinavian countries. Here several languages were being spoken,
obviously closely related, ranging in chronological status from
extremely archaic (Icelandic) to relatively conservative (Swedish)
to greatly modified (Norwegian and Danish). Throughout centuries
the Icelanders had continued to write and speak a language but
little changed since early times, from about the year 1000. Since
the orthography had changed even less than pronunciation, the
people were still able at this time—as indeed they still are today—to
read the poetic and prose texts of their great medieval literature
without any difficulty. This situation meant that continental
Scandinavians had before them a living reminder of what their
own languages must have been like at a time when the differences
between them were negligible, being mere matters of distinction
in local dialects. Moreover, interest was aroused in Old Icelandic
literature for its own sake. The Poetic Edda (11th–13th centuries),
embodying mythological and heroic legends in powerful verse, was
studied and edited and equipped with Latin translations and commentaries in a three-volume edition (Copenhagen 1787–1828). Thus
wider perspectives were opened for European scholarship as
a whole, revealing a very early stage of a single important group
of Northern languages.

At the same time other early Germanic texts were arousing
interest on the continent. A manuscript of the Gothic translation
of the Gospels, made as early as the fourth century, was twice
edited in the 17th. This too was a text of capital importance,
since it revealed a Germanic language in a very early stage of
development. The late 18th century and early 19th witnessed an
upsurge of interest in folklore, especially ballads and *märchen*
(folktales). The collecting of such materials inevitably called attention to the existence of various dialects within a single national
territory, and the awareness of their differences also stimulated
a certain type of linguistic curiosity.

4. The Foundations of Modern Linguistic Science

It was the discovery of the ancient Indian language and literature by Europeans, however, which gave the enormous impetus projecting linguistic studies from the status of amateur speculation to that of a serious discipline. Sir William Jones (1746–94), who had studied such widely diversified languages as Arabic, Hebrew, Persian and Chinese before entering upon his legal training, was sent to India as a judge and there studied Sanskrit, primarily in order to become acquainted with ancient Hindu law. He also read and translated from the ancient Hindu literature. He was the first Western scholar to observe the startling affinity of Sanskrit to both Greek and Latin and to deduce that all three were descended from a common source, probably no longer existent. Following Jones, the brothers August Wilhelm and Friedrich von Schlegel helped to spread the knowledge of this important language and literature in the West, the former by his teaching and translations, the latter especially by his book *Über die Sprache und Weisheit der Indier* (1808).

The time had now come for systematic comparisons and deductions from them. The pioneer study was carried out by a youthful German scholar, Franz Bopp, who at the age of 23 published a monograph comparing the Sanskrit conjugational system with others: *Über das Conjugationssystem der Sanskritsprache in Vergleichung mit jenem der griechischen, lateinischen, persischen und germanischen Sprache* (1816). Bopp's tabulation of verbal endings in several Indo-European languages was enough to indicate clearly their common genetic relationship. Meantime research into early forms of Germanic as compared to the classical languages was bearing fruit. In 1814 a young Danish scholar named Rasmus Rask wrote a monograph (published in 1818) on the origins of early Scandinavian and its relationships with other languages: *Undersøgelse om det gamle nordiske Sprogs Oprindelse*. He pointed out its kinship not only with other Germanic languages and Greek and Latin, but also with the Slavic and Baltic groups. He also noted the regular correspondence of certain initial consonants in the older Germanic dialects, such as Gothic and Old Icelandic, with certain others in related languages outside of the immediate family. Thus if you have Gothic *fadar* and Icelandic *faðir* corresponding to Latin *pater*, Greek πατήρ Sanscrit *pitár*—with initial *p*, you will also expect to find Gothic *fisks*, Icelandic *fiskr*, corresponding to a word like *piscis* in Latin—and you will not be disappointed. If you notice that Gothic and Icelandic have *þu* or *þū* for the second person singular pronoun, preserved in the archaic English *thou*, while Latin has *tū*, you will not be surprised to find forms like Gothic *þrija* (neuter) and modern English *three* corresponding to Latin *trēs* and classical Greek τρεῖς. (The sound represented by *þ* is the one to be heard today at the beginning of words like English *three*, *think*.) Similarly with Germanic *horn* and Latin *cornu*. The tabulation of such correspondences represented a huge step forward in the study of languages which we now know to be related as descendants of an original common ancestor, no longer extant.

It was Jacob Grimm who gave decisive formulation to the principles of correspondence suggested by Rask. While revising the first volume of his *Deutsche Grammatik* (originally published in 1819, second edition 1822), Grimm was able to formulate more clearly, thanks to his reading of Rask, the shifts which must have occurred when the primitive Germanic language was emerging from the original form. For this reason the shift from *p* to *f*, of *t* to *þ*, of *k* to *h* and similar phenomena, is known as Grimm's Law, though Grimm himself would no doubt have been one of the first to acknowledge that he owed much to the work of his predecessors.

Despite the advance represented by Grimm's systematic formulation, however, and the comparative studies of inflexions carried on further by Bopp and his followers, there were many matters which remained unclear. For instance, consonants occurring in the middle of Germanic words were often found to behave otherwise than initial consonants, sometimes conforming to Grimm's formulation, and sometimes not. Such seeming irregularities were at first treated in a rather arbitrary manner, as if they did not deserve serious consideration. Thus the alternation of medial consonants represented in Old High German *slahan*: *gislagen* ("strike: struck"), Modern High German *ziehen*: *gezogen* ("pull: pulled") or Old English *snipan*: *sniden* ("cut: [have] cut") and Modern English *seethe*: *sodden* ("boil: boiled") were at first set aside as irrational variants. But later in the century—in 1875, to be exact— Karl Verner was able to prove that the appearance of a voiced consonant like *g* or *d* in place of an expected voiceless one like *h* or *t* was due to the incidence of prehistoric accent on the words concerned. If a syllable was initial or received primary accent, then Grimm's law held; if not, secondary changes developed which produced voicing of the shifted consonant. (That is to say, a shifted *h* finally became *g*, a *p* was voiced to *ð* and finally became English *d* when primary accent did not protect it from change.) Concomitantly with Verner's great discovery, others were working out the vowel system of the reconstructed parent language. At first scholars had been overly impressed by the pattern of Sanskrit vowels in which *a* occurs with striking frequency. Later it was demonstrated that Sanskrit *a* was not always original, but sometimes represented an earlier front vowel *e*, sometimes a back vowel *o*. The proof lay in the consonants preceding the *a* concerned, for these were sometimes palatalized (that is, pronounced like Modern English *sh* or *ch*, Polish *sz* or *cz*) and sometimes not (that is, retained as *s* or *k*). Obviously, the reason for the different consonants must have lain in the different character of the following vowel, as originally pronounced. We have a similar situation in Modern Italian, where *cinque* is pronounced with a sound resembling modern English *ch* because the so-called front vowel *i* follows it, whereas *colonia* and *cara* are pronounced with a *k*-sound because the so-called back vowels *o* or *a* follow it. The consonant is an index of the nature of the vowel originally following it.

The revisions in the description of prehistoric Indo-European, which was the postulated ancestor language of the Italic, Greek, Germanic, Indic (and Persian), Armenian, Slavic and Baltic languages, led to many stimulating comparative grammars of the then-known languages. Such names as A. Schleicher and A. Pott, G. Curtius and A. Fick are memorable in this connexion. Each

family of languages was found to cast valuable light on the causes
of existing diversities, whether these concerned patterns of altern-
ating accented vowels (as in English *sing, sang, sung*), or reduction
and loss of syllables because of shifted accent (as in Greek πέτομαι
pétomai "I fly" as compared with πτερόν *pterón* "wing, means of
flying") or inflexional endings (well preserved, for instance, in
Modern Lithuanian as well as classical Sanskrit, but reduced in
ancient Greek). As increased knowledge dispelled more and more
obscurities it also revealed orderliness even in those regions where
disorder and arbitrariness had previously appeared to reign.

It is no wonder, then, that linguistic science appeared to resemble
more and more the natural sciences which are capable of strict
formulation in "laws" which admit of no exception. In the 1870's
a number of scholars reached the conclusion that sound changes
occurring throughout the history of a language must be regarded
in the same rigorous fashion: that is to say, an established "law"
like the shift of initial *p* to *f* in early Germanic must be assumed
to have operated universally and consistently at the time when
the change was occurring. Seeming exceptions were to be explained
by the intervention of some other factor, equally capable of
regular and exceptionless explanation. Thus the restricted group
of words in Gothic or Old English or Old Icelandic which do
begin with *p* must have been acquired by these languages, usually
by direct borrowing, after the "law" had ceased to operate. And
it is true that where the etymologies of such words are known,
they turn out to be loans, chiefly from Latin. Thus if the Goths
had borrowed the Latin word *pondus* meaning a pound, at a sufficiently early date, they would inevitably have had to transform it
into something like **funts*[2] instead of keeping the consonants of the
original word. Conversely, the preservation of those consonants
p and *d* is evidence for the chronology of the borrowing: in this
case, after the operation of what we call Grimm's law. Verner's
brilliant demonstration of the regular behaviour of non-initial

---

[2] It is customary to mark with an asterisk * linguistic forms which are
reconstructed on the basis of theory, but which have no historically attested
existence, whether in written or spoken texts.

consonants, despite their seeming capriciousness, served to strengthen the thesis that so-called irregularities merely indicate the existence of a second "law" which must be considered in relation to the first, modifying and conditioning it, if all the pertinent phenomena are to be correctly understood.

It may be said that linguistic science was at this period passing through a phase comparable to that of physical science during the heyday of Newtonian mechanics. The search for universal and exceptionless laws represented an advance over previous methods, in which unguided intuition and guess-work played a great part. But as we shall see (ch. 7) the new method also had its serious limitations.

The school adhering to the slogan of exceptionless linguistic laws is known as that of the Neo-grammarians (German *Neugrammatiker*). Its outstanding exponent was Karl Brugmann (1849–1919), author of an imposing comparative grammar of the Indo-European languages.[3]

Today it is easy for us to criticize the rigorously deterministic formulations of the Neo-grammarians. We have become aware that social phenomena do not lend themselves to descriptions comparable to those of the natural sciences such as physics and chemistry. To cite just one example: the modern investigations into dialects of living languages have revealed that strict boundaries separating one dialect from another are not to be found. An area delimited by one test—for instance the opposition of initial *f*- versus *v*- in English—as in the forms *fly* and *vly*—will be found to be irrelevant for other tests. And within a given area, words of elegant connotation, as used by members of a privileged class,

---

[3] This work, begun in 1886 and finished in 1900, was entitled *Grundriss der vergleichenden Grammatik der indogermanischen Sprachen*. The section on syntax was written by Berthold Delbrück. — It should be noted that the term "Indo-Germanic" is used by German scholars for the family of languages we have been discussing, because they include members extending from ancient India in the East to (Germanic) Icelandic in the West. Other scholars prefer the term "Indo-European," as referring to ancient India plus the entire European continent—or most of it. On non-Indo-European languages in Europe, see ch. 2.

will be found to vary from cognate forms used by the masses of the people as a whole. Urban pronunciation will be found to differ from rural. The two words coming from early Germanic *mūs* and *hūs*, meaning mouse and house respectively, have varying pronunciations in the Netherlandish territory embracing today's Holland and Flanders and extending into Germany. Sometimes the original vowel is preserved in both words, sometimes it is modified in both, and sometimes—this is especially interesting—it is preserved in a word of homely connotations like *mouse* but modified in a word of more sophisticated urban connotations like *house*.

In such situations it is not possible to give a clear, simple and universally applicable formulation of sound changes. Social phenomena require a technique of description appropriate to themselves. Nevertheless the insistence of the Neo-grammarians on rigorous methods and strict discipline was salutary at the time. As a result of their work, many obscure points were illuminated and the comparative study of Indo-European languages, previously marked by inexactitude and guess-work, achieved the dignity of a science.

5. FURTHER ACHIEVEMENTS OF LINGUISTIC SCIENCE

So far we have concentrated attention on the better known languages of the Indo-European family. Old Indian and Hellenic (including the various dialects of ancient Greece), Italic (including Latin and the related dialects of ancient Italy), Germanic, Celtic (including the languages of ancient Ireland and Wales as well as others in the Scottish Highlands and modern Brittany), besides Albanian and Armenian—all these contributed to the picture of a prehistoric language which would explain the discrepancies existing in those historically attested. Some newly discovered languages were also recognized as relatives of the ancient family. Hittite, for instance, although written in cuneiform characters dating from about 1400 B.C., turned out to be a very early relative of other Indo-European languages. Another instance is Tocharian, a language preserved in manuscripts of Eastern Turkestan from the first millenium of our era. Two dialects are represented in these early texts. Curiously enough, they have closer affiliations with Western language groups such as the Italic in Italy or the Celtic in ancient Ireland, than with Eastern groups such as Sanskrit or its close relative Old Persian. The historical connexions of Tocharian still remain somewhat baffling.

The lively interest in languages during the 19th century led to various attempts at the formulation and solution of certain rather theoretical problems. One of them had to do with the ultimate origin of language. Religious dogma had been interpreted to mean that language had been suddenly imparted to man as a divine gift in the not-too-distant past: something like 4000 B.C., according to officially accepted estimates. The multiplicity of existing tongues was explained by the story of the Tower of Babel. Yet it was still assumed that Hebrew, the language of the Old Testament, must somehow stand closer to man's primordial language than any other.

Against such literal interpretations Johann Gottfried Herder raised his voice in a famous essay *On the Origin of Language* (*Über den Ursprung der Sprache*, 1772). In his zeal to refute theories of sudden divine origin, Herder went too far in the opposite direction. He minimized, though he recognized, the differences between animal cries and organized human speech. His anti-theological position, consonant with the attitudes of 18th century rationalism, appears in sentences like this: "It [i.e., the origin of language] is not only not supernatural, but patently animal: the natural law of a sensitive machine." Later the Darwinian theory of biological evolution affected writers on the problem of origins, for instance Heymann Steinthal. Others tried to find the ultimate explanation in primitive forms of inarticulate cries, whether purely imitative (as in English *baa-baa*, supposed to represent the sound emitted by a sheep, and in *cock-a-doodle-doo*, supposed to represent the sound of a cock's crowing)—or already somewhat conventionalized (as when men working together enunciate rhythmical sounds, even today, which cannot be called words). There was also speculation as to whether language had originated at one time and in one place and spread over the inhabited parts of the world (the theory of monogenesis) or had arisen independently in more than one place (the theory of polygenesis). And there were attempts to classify all the languages of the world under a few main headings, either according to their ethno-geographical distribution or according to their internal structure.

Such speculations and efforts were at best premature in the 19th century. Despite intensive work being done on groups of languages previously little known, the amount of information available was insufficient to permit of generalizations. Besides, there is such a vast period of time separating ourselves from the first group (or groups) of speaking human beings that we may never be able to reason our way back to the primeval state of affairs. In this sense no language existing today is really "primitive." Each one of those to which we popularly apply the term in a somewhat condescending spirit, has behind it untold centuries of evolution, in which it could have changed its structure several times over. And the oldest of written records—which are all we have to go by in our attempts to reconstruct extinct or "dead" languages—are the work of but yesterday in comparison with the total span of human history on this planet, as revealed to us in the light of archaeological research.

Theoretical curiosity about the nature and origin of speech was a stimulating factor of importance in the latter 19th century. It led not only to a priori guesses which we now find naive, but also to valuable pioneer work in the investigation of concrete languages and groups of languages outside of those best known in the European area. An attempt will now be made to outline very briefly what we know today about the main families of languages throughout the entire world, and to summarize a few of the more ambitious interpretations of that expanded knowledge.

CHAPTER 2

FAMILIES OF LANGUAGES IN THE WORLD TODAY

1. WHAT IS MEANT BY THE TERM "FAMILY OF LANGUAGES"

As we have seen, the pioneer achievements of linguistic science were realized when scholars began to observe regular correspondences between forms occurring in one European language and those occurring in another: for instance, Latin *tu* corresponding to Polish *ty*, Russian *mu* and English *thou*, etc. The great stimulus afforded by the knowledge of Sanskrit permitted such European scholars to solidify their scheme of relationships and to include within it two Asiatic languages once spoken in ancient Persia and in India. It was the existence of early written records which facilitated more than anything else the establishment of a general scheme of relationships. Once that scheme was charted, then even languages lacking a long history of written records could be analyzed and given a place within the family. The range and wealth of materials available in script favoured the blossoming of linguistic science in Europe, also an atmosphere of intellectual curiosity previously unprecedented. However, this too had its social and historical causes which we understand. It is worth while to emphasize these contributory yet essential conditions, because uninformed persons sometimes assume that pioneer achievements in science—whatever the field—automatically indicate some sort of racial superiority on the part of the pioneers. On the contrary: it appears that with proper materials available (in our case, written records), proper instruction and conditions of work (that is, accessibility to the results of past research and time to make use of them) and a social atmosphere favourable to scientific investigation, any people in any part of the world will be able to carry out some linguistic research. The problem is to create the favourable environment and provide the necessary materials and conditions for work.

[19]

It was in Europe, as it happens, that the techniques were first developed for recognizing relations among languages and grouping them together in families, so-called. European languages, together with their over-seas descendants, were first investigated and for us they are the nearest to home. Therefore we shall begin with them. But first, a few words of explanation and definition are needed.

By a given language we understand a type of oral communication shared and understood by the members of a group of people whether large or small. There are small communities, for instance, on the North and South American continents, where a language is limited to a few hundred speakers, and is said to be dying out. On the other hand there are huge territories, for instance the continent of Australia or Canada and the United States of North America, where a single language predominates. Language and nationality are sometimes but not always associated. A people that have been conquered by a foreign state may cling to their own language and obstinately preserve it even when it is officially suppressed, for the common native tongue becomes a symbol of cultural and national unity persisting in spite of the occupying power. Poland during the Partition and Finland under Tsarist Russia (especially after 1905) are examples in point. On the other hand, however, a single language may be shared by many different nations, as is Spanish in many republics of South America, not to speak of Mexico and Central America as well. And within a single well-organized national state there may exist more than one language enjoying official recognition, as do French, German and Italian in Switzerland, or Flemish and French in Belgium. For a linguist, then, national boundaries are not always of primary importance in classifying his materials.

Besides, it is not easy to draw precise distinctions between languages, whether or not they are associated with separate nations. During the 19th century, when Norway was under the control of Denmark, a literary language called Dano-Norwegian was used for literary composition in both countries. In this language Ibsen wrote his memorable plays. The synthesis was possible because of the marked similarity of modern Danish and Norwegian. To this day, a cultivated speaker of Danish can readily converse with a speaker of Norwegian if each person takes care to enunciate his words clearly and slowly. Nevertheless, there are differences in vocabulary, intonation, pronunciation and so on, which may cause difficulty or misunderstanding. Since Norway won complete political independence the country has standardized its language in its own way, recognizing many features not characteristic of Danish. And so the question arises: is Norwegian a separate language or not? A similar question might be formulated in relation to Flemish, the Germanic language spoken by many citizens of Belgium, and the Dutch which is the language of all of Holland. Anyone who knows Flemish will have no trouble at all in communicating with people he may meet on a journey to Holland. Yet he will also notice differences, especially in vocabulary and pronunciation. Again: one language or two? There is a clear political boundary, but the linguistic boundary is far less clear. In both cases we have to recognize pairs of national languages closely related but nevertheless distinct.

Within a territory that is unified both politically and linguistically there can also be divisions. We all know that dialects exist within national languages. If an originally unified speech community is extended over a sufficiently wide geographical area, internal variations of the language are apt to occur. Sometimes they are minimal, affecting only minor details of pronunciation and vocabulary. But sometimes they are so extensive as to cause difficulty in communication, and even to raise questions of a socio-political character. Such a situation is represented in present-day Scotland within Great Britain. Here there is a local literary language, differing from Standard English of the South but used by many eminent writers from the 14th century down to the present—a language which requires dictionaries and commentaries if it is to be properly understood by readers acquainted only with normal Standard English. The differences resulted from many specific factors: the survival of an early Celtic language in the Scottish Highlands, the exceptionally strong Scandinavian influence in the

North of England, the early development of an Anglo-Saxon dialect characteristic of the North. Hence many striking peculiarities of Modern Scottish, which have engaged the attention of lexicographers, students of comparative grammar, and others. All of these add up to a very specific mode of speaking and writing. But should that mode be designated as a language separate from English? The answer is not easily given. On the one hand there have been centuries of mutual understanding between speakers of English in the far North and in other parts of the country. Yet on the other hand striking differences have developed, as exemplified in the special language used by Robert Burns, besides the language of contemporary poets such as Sir Alexander Gray, Hugh Mac-Diarmid and others. Here, as so often, it is difficult to draw precise boundaries and to discriminate between local dialects on the one hand, and national languages on the other.

For the sake of simplicity, let us assume that a single language is involved, despite minor differences, when speakers of varying backgrounds are able to understand each other without constant reference to a dictionary. In other words, without frequently saying "What's that?—What do you mean by that?" (The statistical frequency of such queries in the case of two similar yet different languages has yet to be established, for instance, in the Scandinavian group.) Thus the English of England and Canada, Australia and the United States, would be recognized as a linguistic unity, despite minor differences; so also the Spanish of Spain and South America, and so on.

But once we have recognized such linguistic unities, we begin to group them together in families. This means nothing more or less than grouping them together according to similar characteristics including the phonological (having to do with the sounds employed in speaking), the morphological (having to do with methods of putting together the elements of speech) and lexicographical (having to do with the words used). On the basis of regularly recurring similarities of various kinds, kinship is recognized, meaning simply that the different languages concerned must have developed out of a previously existing single speech community.

Such terms as "family of languages," "ancestor (or mother) language," "daughter languages," etc. are of course metaphorical. So are other terms that have been used such as the "branching off" of separate languages from a main trunk, as if a tree or a genealogy were involved. However, if one remembers that linguistic evolution is a complex social phenomenon and not a biological one, the metaphor of family relationships can be used safely enough. In the following brief sketch, the more neutral term "related group" will usually be preferred.

2. The Indo-European Group

Most of the territory of Europe and some parts of Asia are occupied today by the very same group of languages which engaged the attention of Bopp and Rask and Grimm and others mentioned in the preceding chapter. This is of course the Indo-European group.

In very ancient times an offshoot of the group was attested in India and Persia. Two languages were derived from this offshoot in the two countries concerned. They were originally so closely similar that they are frequently designated by a single term, Indo-Iranian. But their later histories led, for historical reasons, to a marked divergence. The Iranian branch, originally preserved in two dialect forms (Avestan and Persian), later became diversified and also subjected to outside influences; today the chief Iranian dialect (fārsī) is written in Arabic characters. The Indic branch was first normalized in Sanskrit, the language of ancient religious texts dating from before the ninth century of our era, earlier even than the Persian. These texts represent a language which took shape at a very early time, though in what precise form, we obviously do not know. Recorded forms show obvious kinship with languages in Europe, for instance the words for numerals such as 2 (dvá), 3 (trí), 4 (catvắrah), 5 (páñca) and so on. A speaker of Polish, for instance, will readily observe the resemblance to dwa, trzy, cztery, pięć. Anyone who knows Latin will also observe the resemblance to duo, trēs, quattuor, quinque.

Thus we deduce relationship with languages spoken in Europe at a similarly early time. The ancient Indian language has produced many dialectal descendants, distributed over a wide area of modern India.

One of the closest affiliates of ancient Indian is, curiously enough, a pair of modern North Central European languages, Lithuanian and Lettish. These two are designated by the term Baltic and they form a separate group by themselves, though they occupy a relatively limited geographical area. The neighbouring Slavic group is on the contrary widely extended over Eastern Europe and into Asia. It may be subdivided into three sub-groups: Western (Polish, Czech and Slovak), Southern or Balkan (represented by Bulgarian and Serbo-Croatian, the latter being spoken in Yugoslavia) and Eastern (including Russian, most widely extended of all, and the closely allied White Russian and Ukrainian). Even today the resemblances among members of this great group are clearly visible. The existence of religious texts dating back to the ninth century gives us a basis for reconstructing a picture of the original unified language, Old Slavic, from which the modern national languages have developed. These texts, the work of missionaries from Macedonia, were written in what is generally called Old Church Slavonic or Old Bulgarian.

The main groups thus far mentioned—Indo-Iranian, Baltic and Slavic—are sometimes referred to collectively as the *satem* languages. The reason for this is that a number of words in all of them have hissing or "sibilant" consonants like *s*, whereas obviously cognate words in other groups clearly show an original *k*-sound. The word *satem* itself is Old Persian for 100, and it corresponds to Russian and Polish *sto*, Lithuanian *szìmtas*, whereas Latin has *centum*; Greek has *katón* (with the prefix *he-*) and Old Irish has *cēd*, all with initial *k*-sound. Compare also Polish *serce* with Latin *cord-is* for the same sort of contrast.

The reason for the change of pronunciation in the former instances was the fact that the original *k*- once common to all, was apparently enunciated from a point relatively high in the mouth: as in the English word *kin*, for instance, as contrasted with *cool*, which has an initial *k*- sound enunciated farther back. In the former case the *k*- is said to be fronted. All languages of the so-called *satem* groups transformed these fronted consonants (but not the others) into sibilants, while languages of the so-called *centum* groups did not. It may be pointed out that the same sort of change occurred in the Latin word itself at a much later date, when it developed into French *cent*, with an initial *s*- sound.

For this reason it has been supposed that the division here indicated corresponds to an early separation of the primitive lost language, ancestor of all of them, into an Eastern dialect and a Western. However, other tests produce divisions which cut across this classification, and it is by no means sure just what historical interpretation should be given to any one of them, taken by itself.

Returning now to the survey of the major groups, we find one that played an outstanding role in ancient times and has had an unbroken if varied history down to the present. This is the Hellenic group. In antiquity it embraced a number of distinct Greek dialects, of which Attic, the one used in Athens, played a leading role for political and cultural reasons. The world of the Eastern Mediterranean for a long time used Greek as an international means of communication. The high quality of Greek literature and Greek education naturally increased its prestige.

A second major group emerged into prominence somewhat later, namely the Italic. Like Greece, ancient Italy at one time showed a diversity of related forms of speech. Two of them, Oscan and Umbrian, are preserved on inscriptions which permit us to gain some impression of their linguistic structures. But it was Latin, of course, which supplanted its rivals (both related and unrelated), not only in the peninsula itself but throughout most of the then known world. It was the vehicle for a distinguished literature, but it was also the instrument of government and military organization throughout a huge empire. As is natural, however, the language of buyers and sellers in the market place, of ordinary soldiers and workers, differed from that of the highly cultivated writers of epic poems, orations and histories. Besides, Latin was learned as a second language by inhabitants of provinces which were conquered territories. Thus two types of differentiation arose. The first was the contrast between "classical" and "popular" Latin, observable in Italy itself. It was the latter form which was carried to the provinces by ordinary soldiers, emigrés, commercial travellers and the like. The second differentiation was due to the contact of Latin with various types of native languages in provinces extending from Britain to Africa and Asia Minor. The result was a wide range of local nuances. In specific areas these gave rise in the course of centuries to a series of subgroups including some leading national languages today. They are, ranging from East to West, Rumanian, Italian, French (extending into Switzerland and Belgium), Spanish and Portuguese. The last two are also widely spoken in the New World. Collectively all are known as the Romance languages. There are also specific forms of Romance which are themselves quite distinct linguistically but do not coincide with national boundaries: for instance, Catalan in Spain and Provençal in France. Their close kinship will be noticed by anyone who studies them even on the most elementary level.

The Roman Empire, as is well known, succumbed to a series of attacks by outside peoples, most of whom spoke very closely related languages. In the fifth century, so far as we can surmise, one might well have called them related dialects. The Huns, led by Attila, were an exception. Their language was quite separate from that of other invaders, but the others were clearly developed from a common source. They are collectively designated as General Germanic. Their source (not extant in writing, but fairly well indicated by surviving evidence) is called Primitive Germanic. We are greatly assisted in envisaging its nature by the existence of the fourth-century Biblical translation into Gothic, a language now extinct.

The Germanic group today occupies a considerable territory and embraces several national languages. These may for convenience be separated into Scandinavian and non-Scandinavian. The former sub-group, sometimes called North Germanic, exhibits many common traits, although its modern representatives vary greatly. Icelandic, as has been pointed out (ch. 1, sec. 4), is by far the most archaic and conservative in matters of vocabulary. Swedish occupies a middle position, while Danish and Norwegian show the greatest innovations in structure and pronunciation. Outside of Scandinavia, Germanic languages are spoken in England, Belgium, Switzerland, Germany and Austria. They are commonly referred to as West Germanic. Here too there are many common traits, but there are also marks of differentiation. One of them is the treatment of certain consonants. For instance, cognates of the English word *deep* also have an initial *d-* in Flemish, Dutch, and dialects spoken in the Northern (low-lying) parts of Germany. On the other hand the corresponding word in literary German (which developed in the more Southerly, high-lying parts, including Austria) has an initial *t-* (*tief*). Many such regular correspondences lead to a classification of the non-Scandinavian sub-group into Low and High German. The term is purely geographical and has obviously nothing to do with moral or aesthetic values, as is sometimes supposed.

Still another group, the Celtic, was at one time an important member of the Indo-European family. It was spoken in territories extending from present-day Czechoslovakia through Austria, Southern Germany, Northern Italy, France, and the British Isles. Traces of it are to be found in Asia Minor. Today the survivals of Celtic are greatly restricted. They fall into two sub-groups. One of them exists on the West Coast of Ireland and in the Northern Highlands of Scotland. The second exists in Wales and in the French province of Brittany. Both branches are enormously interesting for specialists, and both have valuable early texts, Irish yielding the oldest. But the divergence between the branches has gone very far in pronunciation as well as other matters. To cite but one example: where the common Indo-European ancestor language appears to have had a sound like k^w, represented in Latin by *qu-* (compare the Modern English pronunciation of the word *quiet*), the Old Irish and its derivative Highland Scottish (or Gaelic) show a simple *k*, whereas Welsh and Breton show *p*. Thus Latin *quattuor*, meaning four, corresponds to Irish *cathir* (with initial *k-*) but to Welsh *pedwar*. For this reason the two sub-groups are sometimes called Q-Celtic and P-Celtic.

Among living languages there are two isolated ones: Albanian and Armenian, which clearly belong to the Indo-European group, though both have been subjected to many alien influences which somewhat obscure their filiation. Old Armenian is attested in early religious writings. Derived forms of it are spoken in Asia Minor (Southeast of the Black Sea), in the Soviet Republic of Armenia and in scattered territories of other republics. The development of consonants in Armenian shows a curious parallelism with that known to us in early Germanic. Albanian is attested only since early modern times and because of its complex ingredients and modified character it was one of the last European languages to be correctly classified. Both Albanian and Armenian are, in traditional terminology, *satem* languages.

Among the Indo-European languages no longer spoken, some are known to us from inscriptions (for instance, Thracian and Phrygian) or rare manuscripts (for instance Tocharian in Central Asia; see p.16f.). Ancient Hittite, the language of a people frequently mentioned in the Biblical Old Testament, is preserved in numerous cuneiform inscriptions discovered in present-day Turkey and deciphered early in the present century. This was obviously a very ancient representative of the Indo-European group. One specialist at least has argued that Hittite was not actually a member of that group, but a related co-equal, so that we should speak of a period of prehistoric unity in which Hittite and ancestral Indo-European were related much as prehistoric Baltic and Slavic, Italic and Celtic and Germanic were related. But it is difficult to establish precise relationships on the basis of limited materials surviving from a very early period.

3. FINNO-UGRIC AND BASQUE

Within modern Europe there are several representatives of a group quite distinct from Indo-European which must at one time have occupied a considerable territory in the Northern part of the Eurasian continent. It is represented by three national languages: Finnish (or Suomi), Estonian and Hungarian. Linguistically the first two represent a unity while Hungarian or Magyar is rather separate. Related tongues are spoken by communities scattered over a wide area in Northern Europe and East and Southeast of the Ural Mountains: for instance Lappish (in the North of Norway, Sweden and Russia), forms of Ugrian, Permian and Samoyed in Northern Siberia. Hungarian is geographically separated from other members of the group because of a long migration leading to final settlement in the Danube region in the ninth century. The entire group is usually called Finno-Ugric. Despite early separations and far-flung migrations the members show striking similarities to this day, so that it is possible to deduce many of the characteristics of the common language from which all of them sprang. One of the most striking of them is a trait of pronunciation known as vowel harmony. This means that if a word begins with a syllable containing a vowel of a certain character—say a vowel articulated in the front part of the mouth like, *i, e,* or German *ü*—then all of the vowels in succeeding syllables must have a similar articulation. Conversely, if the word begins with a vowel of contrasting character—say one with back articulation like *a, o, u*—then all the succeeding syllables must likewise have similar vowels. In practice this means that whenever a suffix is added to a word there must be alternate forms available so that the harmony or correspondence may be carried through. Thus in Hungarian the plural of *bolt* meaning shop is *boltok*, while the plural of *eb* meaning dog is *ebek*: an example of choice between *-o-k* and *-e-k* as sign of the plural number. The principle has been variously adapted and often obscured in the various living languages, but its early existence is clear. Sometimes a series of "neutral" vowels is recognized which may appear with either series indifferently.

Another striking characteristic is that words are modified by a process of agglutination, as it is called, rather than inflexion. The boundary between the two is not easily defined, but it may be explained in simple terms somewhat like this. In inflected languages, represented especially in the older forms of Indo-European, the relation of one word to another in a sentence was habitually expressed by a colourless suffix which could not function as a word by itself. Thus in the English phrase *my father's house*, the *-s* after *father*, meaningless if spoken by itself, is understood to indicate a relationship of possession just as if one had said *the house belonging to my father*. It is the same with the *-a* of Polish *ojca* in the phrase *dom ojca*; with the *-is* of Latin *patris* in the phrase *patris domus*. Other relationships are expressed in a similarly abstract manner. But it is possible to get the same effect of relationship if one attaches words (or reduced forms of words) after one another: thus in a garbled but still understandable form of English, *house-belong-father* or even *house 'long father*; *bed-to* instead of *to bed* (Polish *łóżka-do* instead of *do łóżka*). The latter procedure can be observed in the Finno-Ugric languages. Thus many relationships which are expressed elsewhere by means of prepositions such as English *beyond* or Polish *za*, and by possessive pronouns, are here indicated by agglutinated postpositions: thus in Finnish the expression meaning outside your hut appears as *kodastanne*, where *koda* = hut, *-sta* = outside and *-nne* = your. There are however a number of postpositional elements which function precisely as inflexional endings, since they have been reduced to syllables no longer revealing their origin (if such it was) in independent words. In this sense, therefore, it would be unsafe to classify the Finno-Ugric languages as exclusively agglutinating.

The Basque language has been included in this section, not because it has any visible relationship with any of those so far discussed, but merely because it is the only other distinctive type of speech to be found on the continent of Europe today. It is spoken in the Pyrenees area, mostly in Spain but partly in France. The Basque vocabulary shows no relationship with that of any European neighbour, and words are put together in sentences in a manner unparalleled elsewhere. It is thought that the language represents the survival from an extremely ancient prehistoric speech community, long antedating the arrival of speakers of Indo-European (such as the Celts) in the Iberian peninsula. Some scholars have tried to establish the affinity of Basque with groups as diverse and remote as Japanese and American Indian, not to speak of Etruscan (an extinct non-Indo-European language of ancient Italy about which we know very little). All we can say is that in the absence of early records we simply do not have enough evidence to reach any conclusions in the matter.

4. SEMITIC-HAMITIC

In ancient times the languages of two related sub-groups, today called Semitic and Hamitic respectively, played a very important part as the vehicles of highly civilized cultures. In the region of the Tigris and Euphrates Rivers the Assyrians and Babylonians, representing the first sub-groups, succeeded in establishing, in the third millenium before our era, imposing empires about which we know very much because of the abundant archaeological remains. Moreover, they left many written records, preserved in cuneiform inscriptions chiseled on stone or scratched on clay tablets. Their alphabet is called cuneiform because it is make up of configurations of wedge-like strokes arranged in conventional patterns. This alphabet has long since been deciphered, and we know the words it recorded. Closely related to these two languages, jointly known as Akkadian, was ancient Hebrew, spoken in a relatively tiny area once called Palestine or Judaea. The importance of Hebrew became gigantic in the history of human culture because of the role played by its sacred books, commonly known as the Old Testament of the Bible (Biblia). After the collapse of the originally independent state of Judaea under Roman domination, the ancient tongue was preserved by scattered communities in connexion with religious studies and observances. Recently, after World War II, this classical Semitic tongue has been revived and established as a living national language in Israel, and its internal resources have been developed to provide a vocabulary adequate for the needs of a modern technological civilization. Aramaic, a language related to Hebrew, spread widely after about 300 B.C., but is long since extinct.

Arabic, a close relative of Hebrew, was originally spoken in the area lying South of Asia Minor, between the Red Sea and the Gulf of Aden. It became the language of Mohammedan Islam, which in the early Middle Ages extended its political conquests and religious communities over a wide territory including original Arabia, Northern Africa and Spain. It produced an abundant literature of creative imagination and scholarly research, and today it is the language of many peoples dwelling in a roughly semicircular band of territories extending from Arabia, Iraq and Syria in the East through Egypt and across North Africa and down along its Northwest coast. A Semitic language of some importance in ancient times, now extinct, was Phoenician, spoken in Asia Minor.

The second subgroup, namely the Hamitic, had its most famous ancient representative in Egypt, with a civilization reflected in writings that go back as far as three millenia before our era. (The terms Semitic and Hamitic, by the way, are derived from the names of two sons of Noah in the Bible, Sem or Shem and Ham, supposed to have been the progenitors of the two families of peoples concerned.) A continuation of the ancient tongue, known as Coptic, was used for early Christian literature in Egypt, but it was soon overshadowed by Arabic and passed out of living use. A close neighbour of Old Egyptian was Cushite, spoken over a large area to the Southeast. (This term also comes from the Bible.) Modern Hamitic languages are varied and occupy a wide territory in Northern and Central Africa. An outstanding example is Ethiopian in Abyssinia, surrounded by modern Cushite dialects to the North and South. Across Northern Africa, Berber speech communities also represent Hamitic, and there are many other related dialects in central Africa.

Throughout the course of history much differentiation has of course appeared within the two subgroups, so that today their genetic relationship is far from obvious. But if we go back to the earliest records, certain similarities become clearly apparent. Members of the Semitic subgroup have vocabularies sharing very many common elements and they also show many similar characteristics in morphology, syntax and word order. A striking trait common to Hebrew and Arabic, for instance, is the predominance of word roots based on three consonants. By varying the vowels between such consonants, and by adding prefixes and suffixes, all sorts of linguistic relations can be indicated on the basis of a single root: noun versus verb, one tense versus another, singular versus plural. An example would be the hypothetical triliteral root *mlk*, with the general meaning of reigning or ruling, from which could be derived terms meaning a ruler or forms of the verb to rule, etc., and by compounding also: father (son) of the ruler. (Note that in Hebrew the -*k* became -*ch*, standing for a sound pronounced roughly as in modern German or Polish. Compare the Biblical names Abimelech and Melchisedech.) Triliteral roots also prevail in Egyptian and the Berber dialects. Although duoliteral roots based on two consonants only are in the majority in modern Cushite, comparative studies seem to indicate that these originated in earlier triconsonantal forms. Thus there is good reason to postulate an original Semitic-Hamitic unity of speech, although specialists are understandably cautious in expressing opinions in this matter.

5. ALTAIC (URAL-ALTAIC) AND PALEO-SIBERIAN

The term Altaic is somewhat misleading. Derived from the name of the Altai Mountains in Central Asia, it implies a related speech community embracing not only modern Turkish and its obvious relatives, but also Mongol and Tunguz. The territory is very extensive in the geographical sense and also diversified linguistically. The Turkic subdivision, as we shall call it here for convenience's sake, now covers a huge area comparable to that of today's Semito-Hamitic. In the Northeast of Siberia the Yakut language is spoken along two sections of the Lena River and in scattered territories to the East. In the Southwest of Siberia we find a whole cluster of languages (or should we say dialects?) including Kazak, Uzbek, Uigur, Turkmen and others. These include territories adjacent to the Ural Mountains as well as the Volga River. Turkian or Turkish proper is the national language of Turkey and is spoken outside of the country as well, not only in Asia Minor but also in limited areas at the mouth of the Danube and along the shores of the Bosphorus. At one time Turkish prevailed over a considerable European territory, including the Balkans and Hungary, but has in modern times become restricted almost entirely to the continent of Asia.

Among the Turkic languages, a number of fundamental similarities testify to close relationship. Here again, as in Finno-Ugric, we find the principle of vowel harmony, this time applied according to an even more subtle and complicated ʹsystem, being based on more than one contrast in the manner of articulation. Inflectional and derivational suffixes added to simple or "root" forms are in each case clearly developed from a single source, whether it is a question of case endings or conjugational endings or suffixes indicating nominal forms of the verb.

Mongol and Tunguz, covering an extensive area in Central Asia and Siberia, show many traits of similarity with general Turkic. These traits include the use of vowel harmony, much coincidence of vocabularies, and syntactic patterns. The resemblances in morphology (that is, the arrangement of elements which go into the formation of words) are however apparently minimal. For this reason—since the principles of word formation by means of suffixes and the like are very important in establishing linguistic relationships—specialists hesitate to assign Mongol and Tunguz to the same major group as Turkic. Vocabulary, as is well known, is very easily borrowed, for instance as a result of conquest or close cultural relations. The influx of French words into English (and also into Polish, though here to a less degree) is a case in point. Pronunciation and syntactic organization of sentences may also be affected. The Asiatic peoples here concerned moved about widely in early times and often had occasion to adopt alien tongues. In the absence of early written documents it is thus difficult to be sure of ultimate genetic relationships, and the question remains an open one.

At this point it will be convenient to mention some neighbours of Tunguz located mainly to the Northeast on the Chukotsk and Kamchatka peninsulas. The dialects are designated as Paleo-Siberian, since they seem to represent survivals of an early language originally widely extend over Northern Siberia. They are however quite unconnected with either Turkic or Mongol or Tunguz. Picture-writing had been developed by the eastern-most tribes, but a modified form of the Russian alphabet has been adopted for school instruction under the auspices of the educational program of the Soviet Union.

6. Sino-Tibetan and Its Neighbours

Chinese, a language of ancient literary traditions, is spoken today by a huge number of people (over 600 million within the People's Republic of China, not to mention colonies of residents outside its boundaries). It would perhaps be more accurate to speak of Chinese as a cluster of similar languages rather than a single one, since speakers from one province are often quite unable to understand those from another. Nevertheless there are many common traits pointing to close relationship and an ultimate single origin. It is possible to deduce the outstanding characteristics of archaic Chinese by a study of the forms existing today.

Very striking in all forms of contemporary Chinese is the predominance of monosyllabic words arranged in sentences in such a way that their relationship is indicated primarily by position. To speakers of a highly inflected Indo-European language such as Polish, this fashion of expressing oneself may seem strange. (It will seem less strange to a speaker of English, which also relies to a great extent on word order rather than grammatical inflections.) But Chinese has not lacked techniques of compounding and deriving word-elements, even though the process is not always clearly perceptible in the resulting morphological units. Today's monosyllables, in other words, may be the result of a complicated process of evolution. Besides, Chinese makes use of musical values (pitch) in order to discriminate the very many words that would otherwise be homonyms. It is as if English were to distinguish *be* (the verb) from *bee* (the insect) by giving the first a low pitch and the second a high one, the same with Polish *pory* ("seasons") and *pory* ("leeks"). In view of the diversity of speech communities in present-day China, the traditional use of an ideographic system of writing has a considerable value for purposes of communication. The manifold characters originally based on picture writing but later stylized and much diversified do not represent sounds so much as concepts. Hence ideograms conveying the sense of *man*, *city*, *within* will be understood in all parts of the Chinese-speaking world, even though individual groups attach differing phonetic values to the signs concerned.

The Tibetan and Burmese languages belong to a related group, spoken in an extensive area between India and China, formerly called Indo-China. They share common phonetic characteristics and methods of word derivation by means of prefixes and suffixes. There is a probable relation with Chinese, but it is by no means clear. Among the curious traits of Tibetan is the essentially impersonal treatment of the verb, which is handled without personal subjects as we understand the term. This means that an action or a condition of being seems to be conceived in the abstract, and its relation to performers or receivers must be expressed by other means than conjugation as we understand the term. Aspects are distinguished rather than temporal relationships. Moreover, the distinction between what we call noun and verb was by no means rigid, especially in early times—just as it is not rigid in Modern English in very many cases. (The same impersonal treatment of the verb, the stress on aspect and lack of formal distinction between noun and verb are to be found, by the way, in the Thai family of what was once French Indo-China.) Burmese has undergone more changes than conservative Tibetan, partly due to the greater influence of Old Indian upon it.

The Korean speech community borders on the Chinese to the South-east. Although quite independent, it shows some analogies with Tibetan and Burmese, for instance in its treatment of verbs, which are indifferent to categories of person and number. There are however various types of suffixes which indicate what we would call tense and aspect. Special nuances of politeness may be expressed in verb-forms, and these serve in a way to replace pronominal functions. Their origin and function are clearly related to a social structure based on many gradations of class relationships.

Japanese is again quite separate from all the languages just discussed. Its alphabet represents an adaptation of Chinese characters to record an entirely different vocabulary and grammatical structure. One of the striking characteristics of Japanese is the great preponderance of open syllables (that is, syllables ending in a vowel). For this reason, when the English word *ground* is borrowed in the sense of sports terrain, it becomes *gu.ra.u.n.do*, thus avoiding the consonant clusters of the original. Like Korean, Japanese makes abundant use of suffixes and enclitics, and yet its verbal and nominal forms are similarly neutral as to categories of person and number. "Politeness" verbs play a role similar to that found in Korean. There are many homonymic words and root-forms in Japanese, but variations in musical pitch are not used (as in Chinese) to differentiate them.

Malay-Polynesian is a term applied to a chain of languages embracing such wide-spread territories as Madagascar, the Malay peninsula, Indonesia, New Zealand and the far-sundered islands in the Pacific. Though there are differences in the phonetic systems, the similarities in vocabulary, in the use of suffixes and in sentence structure, are obvious to the least trained observer. The close relationship of Indonesian tongues among themselves may be illustrated by the words for the number 5: *limi* in Madagascar, *lima* in Malayan and Javanese. As for the languages in the Polynesian group, spoken throughout islands of the Pacific, including New Zealand, they show obvious similarities with the Indonesian group, but have eliminated a number of consonants which must have existed in the common parent language. As a result, the Polynesian dialects depend greatly on vowels and relatively little on consonants for the phonetic material of words. The close relationship with the Indonesian group appears in words like *lima, rima* and *ima,* here also meaning five. Throughout the Malay-Polynesian community words are readily juxtaposed and compounded, but without inflexions as these are understood in Indo-European. An example is the familiar Malay loanword *orang-utan,* literally meaning man [of] jungle: that is, wild man.

Similar is *mata-hari*, literally eye [of] day (compare English *daisy* from *day's eye*).

The Australian native languages, largely displaced by English, are a family in themselves, so far little studied.

Within the huge territory of Asia and islands to the East of it there are various smaller families, interesting in themselves, which for reasons of space cannot be discussed here even briefly. Two larger families remain to be mentioned, at least in passing.

Dravidian is the name applied to a group of closely related languages spoken in Southern India, including Tamil, Telugu, Kanara and others. In earlier times, Dravidian must have occupied a much greater territory, but was pushed southwards and restricted by the invading speakers of Indo-European (Old Indian). Dravidian has many interesting traits of its own. Though it lacks prefixes and infixes it makes use of various kinds of suffixes. Among these is a curious system of inflexion for nouns according as they refer to "superior" beings (gods, demons, men) or "inferior" beings (animals and non-living objects), with females—whether human or divine—variously classified and treated in the separate languages.

Caucasian seems to refer to a geographical rather then a linguistic entity. Within the area of the Caucasus Mountains a great diversity of tongues is to be found. Those to the North, including Cherkes, are clearly related with one another. The filiations of those to the South are much more problematical. Among the latter, Georgian has the oldest written literature and is spoken by the greatest number of people, residing between the Black Sea and the Caspian.

7. AFRICAN GROUPS TODAY

As has already been indicated in section 3, Semitic and Hamitic languages are spoken throughout a large part of Northern Africa. But other important families occupy the central and Southern parts of that vast continent.

In a wide belt stretching across Northern Africa, bounded on the South by a line extending Eastwards from the shores of the

Gulf of Guinea and then dipping still farther to the South, we find a chain of languages grouped together and known as Sudanese-Guinean. Some but not all of them use variations of tone (musical pitch) to distinguish words and word-forms: thus in Ewe, a part of the Ivory-Dahoman subgroup, the word *ka* with low tone means to scatter, while *ka* with high tone means to touch. The use of prefixes and suffixes is widespread. The former indicate classes of nouns, aspects of verbs and the like; but suffixes are also used to indicate nominal classes (e.g. in Voltaic), plurality and some conjugational forms of verbs. The prefixes and suffixes may resemble those appearing in Indo-European languages to a certain extent but their role is often quite different. They frequently express relationships not familiar to the languages of Europe.

South of the Sudanese-Guinean family, the Bantu family occupies a wide territory in Central Africa. Its members possess many common traits, and it also shows kinship with its Northern neighbours in the Sudano-Guinea area. Here too we find noun classes distinguished by prefixes which are sometimes echoed throughout a sentence. The repetition serves to reaffirm the class of the subject-noun in the following words connected with it, such as demonstratives, adjectives and so on. For example in this sentence from a language of the Congo: *Ba-leke ba-na ba mfumu, ba-nkaka ba mbote ba-nkaka ba mbi, ba-fwi idi ba-akulu*; literally "Boys—those of the chief, the ones good the others bad, they died all of them." The insistent repetition of *ba-* is obvious. Infixes and suffixes are also widely used. Many roots of words are common to all the Bantu groups, as can be seen at a glance by comparing key words taken for instance from the number system or the lists of personal pronouns. E.g., the absolute form of the first personal pronoun in languages from eleven widely distributed groups appears as follows: *mina, mema, mimi, nene, nze, owami, mono, mba, ma, emi, mbi.*

Khoin is the term now generally applied to the South African native languages. They fall into two main groups, Bushman and Hottentot, quite unrelated to Sudanese-Bantu. A striking feature of all of them is the use of several distinct sounds called clicks, which are based on a sucking-in of the air instead its expulsion. Combined with other speech sounds in the respective languages, they lend to them a very special auditory character.

8. AMERINDIAN FAMILIES

The term Amerindian has been invented by specialists to cover all the native languages of the Western Hemisphere; it is convenient because it avoids any possible confusion with Indian as applied to some languages of Southern Asia. However, the term should not be understood to imply any sort of linguistic unity observable today. Actually, the American continents contain very many different languages (about 100, it is roughly estimated), not to speak of dialects. Before the arrival of the white colonists there must have been very many more.

The question of origins and of connexions with linguistic families in the Old World has often been raised. Some specialists have claimed kinship for one group or another with such families as Ural-Altaic, Sino-Tibetan or Malay-Polynesian; others find the offered evidence unconvincing. If, as seems likely, human beings first came to the New World—until that time unpopulated—by crossing the Bering Strait into Alaska, this must have occurred in ages so very remote in pre-history that we can no longer trace the circumstances. We do not know, for one thing, whether the immigrants came in waves carrying forms of a single very primitive language, or languages already distinct at that time. The many millenia that elapsed before the 16th century would in any event have given opportunity for vast differentiations in speech, the more so since very many of the tribes continued to follow a nomadic way of life which favoured cultural isolation.

Unfortunately the Amerindian languages did not attract the attention of linguists until modern times: about the turn of the present century. In the meantime many must have died out because of neglect, not to speak of a frequent policy of downright extermination on the part of the conquerors. Recently however some excellent studies have been made, especially of languages surviving in the United States, Mexico and Central America. A pioneer in the field was Franz Boas, an American anthropologist who realized (as did many of his colleagues and followers) that knowledge of a native's language is indispensable if one is to study his culture as a whole. Thus Amerindian linguistic science is indebted in the first place to anthropologists rather than to professional linguists in the strict sense of the word.

Boas himself warned against premature attempts to classify the Amerindian languages in families or super-families. Nevertheless one of his successors, the distinguished scholar Edward Sapir, attempted to do so. He suggested six "stocks" for a huge territory in the North American continent, extending from the extreme North of Canada down into Mexico (though not including all of that country). Though doubtful as a linguistic classification, according to present opinion, the six stocks offer a convenient series for a geographical survey of the varied materials now at our disposal. They are, following Sapir:

(1) Eskimo-Aleutian, spoken from the Aleutian Islands across Northern Canada and in Greenland. This stock engaged the attention of linguists at a relatively early period (e.g. Rasmus Rask in Denmark), and connexions with Northern Siberian languages have been suggested.

(2) Algonquin-Wakash prevailing across the entire continent in Southern Canada and the Northern United States.

(3) Hoka-Siou, found in a large territory extending from the Northern United States as far as Mexico (Lower California, and, on the opposite side, a Northeastern area of Mexico).

(4) Na-Dene, occupying areas in Northwestern Canada and along the West Coast of Canada and the United States.

(5) Penutia, occupying relatively restricted areas on the West Coast from British Columbia and Oregon into California.

(6) Uto-Aztec-Tono, representing an extensive, North-South band in the Western United States, passing into central Mexico and continued, in spots at least, as far as Panama.

Of the stocks listed above, the last-named is most interesting for students of pre-Columbian history and culture in the New World, because it includes Nahuatl, the language (existing today in various dialects) which had achieved great prestige just before the arrival of the Spaniards in Mexico. It was the official language of the Aztec empire centered in today's Mexico City. Nahuatl was recorded for practical purposes by Spanish missionaries in the 16th century, but a scientific analysis has only recently been achieved. The range of its sounds is limited, but it makes extensive use of prefixes, infixes and suffixes to express morphological relationships, especially in the verbal system.

Maya-Soke (or Zoque) is an outstanding family, the most important of Southern Mexico and Central America. Maya proper was the language of an imposing pre-Columbian civilization established in Yucatan and adjacent areas, where it survives to a certain extent today. Its close relative Quiché was associated with a similar advanced civilization in Guatemala. The architectural monuments of the Aztec, Maya and Quiché regions—palaces, pyramids, temples—although now in ruins, remain as testimony to the high artistic and technical achievements of the indigenous peoples.

Arawak is a family of native languages spoken in the Antilles and it probably extended at one time over the Northern parts of South America as well. Carib belongs in the region North of the Amazon; and there are many other families of native languages in South America, hitherto little investigated. Kichua, spoken formerly throughout the empire of the Peruvian Incas, was associated like Nahuatl and Maya with imposing achievements in art, material culture and political organization. Since it was widely used outside of Peru itself, Kichua was early studied by Spanish missionaries and used as a means of instruction and religious conversion over a wide territory.

9. SOME GENERAL PROBLEMS

Even this brief and incomplete survey will have indicated how very numerous and diversified are the types of languages spoken on our planet today. Within the brief scope of recorded history we have abundant evidence for the various ways in which individual languages may be extended to ever wider territories at the expense of others. The usual method of expansion has been by conquest and colonization. An invading people brings with it an alien speech, let us say, which is imposed from above upon the conquered. The latter may continue to communicate among themselves as previously, but must perforce learn the language of the strangers. Sometimes, depending on social and economic relations between conquerors and conquered, a language of mixed character may evolve, as was the case in medieval England. Sometimes the conquerors' language wins out completely, yet in the process it nevertheless takes on some features of the one subdued and displaced. In such a situation we speak of the substratum or underlying layer in relation to the superstratum or dominant layer. Much depends on the degree of cultural contact between the two. In North America (Canada and the United States) for instance, the white settlers remained aloof and hostile towards the natives, hence the borrowings from the latter into English were limited to geographical place-names and a small number of nouns.

A single language extended by conquest or otherwise over a large territory may in the end develop into many languages for various reasons. One of the clearest examples of this is the popular or colloquial Latin of the Roman Empire (see above, p. 26). Because we have written records for Latin and the Romance languages covering more than 2000 years, we are able to trace the development fairly clearly. In other cases we have to surmise on the basis of much scantier evidence. However, the study of local dialects within the confines of a single national language can often illustrate in contemporary terms how differentiations arose in early times, even in prehistory.

A question that has been asked more than once is this: Did human speech have a single origin, or several independent origins? (See ch. 1, sec. 5.) Certain writers, some of them under the influence of Christian fideism, have inclined to stress whatever evidence is available for the hypothesis of a single origin (monogenesis) of speech. Others have argued for multiple origin (polygenesis) of speech for different reasons. All that we can say is that our present knowledge, wide as it is, does not extend to the kind of prehistorical materials which would permit of a satisfactory answer to the question.

Another question has been asked, and some writers have attempted to answer it. The question is: Can the languages of the world be classified under a few convenient categories, according to their morphological structures? A rough classification sometimes proposed is the following:

(1) Isolating or analytic languages, in which uninflected simple forms are juxtaposed;

(2) Agglutinating languages, in which forms are loosely strung together to form units;

(3) Inflectional or synthetic languages in which prefixes and suffixes (sometimes infixes) are merged with roots into single complex forms.

But on closer observation it turns out that no such classification is possible. Many and various are the devices used to express linguistic relations, and many combinations of devices are to be found in the world's languages today. The factors are so numerous, and our knowledge as yet so limited, that we cannot risk generalizations with regard to such matters.

CHAPTER 3

WORDS AND WORD FORMATION

1. Free and Bound Elements in Words

If someone who is not a linguistic expert is suddenly asked, "What are the elementary units employed by the speakers of a language?" he will no doubt reply without hesitation, "Why, words of course!" And he will point to an up-to-date dictionary and say: "There you have all the units, conveniently arranged and explained."

But a moment's reflection will show that the matter is really not so simple as all that. Especially if we go by written forms alone, we may wonder from time to time how the decision is made about the identification of words as units and the drawing of boundaries between them. English is particularly baffling in this respect. Anyone can see that the word *nevertheless* is made up of three units which also exist independently in the language, namely *never+the+less*. So also with French *parceque* (*par+ce+que*) and German *heutigen+tags* (*heutigen+Tag(e)s*). We observe in such cases a process of grouping separate, still recognizable forms together to constitute a new unity. One can analyze such combinations readily. Others are less obvious. In the English word *together*, for instance, the first element *to-* is easily recognized upon a moment's reflection as identical with the *to-* in the word *today* or in the phrase *run to cover*. But the second element, namely *–gether* is not as easily recognized as a variant of the familiar word *gather*, which it is. Similarly the speakers of English may be more or less aware that in the word *because* the second element is the familiar word *cause*, but fail to see in the first element an unaccented variant of the preposition *by*. Examples could be multiplied. Polish has words like *zamiast* and *natomiast* in which the first elements (*za*, *na*, *to*) exist also as separate words while the final one does not. Yet although there is no such word as *miast[1] in Polish, this word elemnet can also be related (like English -gether) to a well-known term, namely miasto, meaning city; and this in turn has a fairly clear connexion with miejsce meaning place (compare Russian место). Moreover the separate Polish word meaning not, namely nie, is also recognizable as a negative prefix appearing in many words. For instance niegrzeczny (literally, not polite; hence rude, disrespectful or—when applied to children—naughty).

But there may also be elements in words which, though often recurrent and therefore recognizable as individual units in the vocabulary of a language, having definable functions attached to them, nevertheless are not to be found in independent positions, even in a modified form. Thus the English negative prefix un-, unlike the Polish nie-, can never appear alone. It cannot constitute the reply to a question. It is always attached to another element to form a linguistic unity. Thus in English one may say "I am unhappy", but never "I un-am happy." Yet in Polish one can say either Jestem nieszczęśliwy or Nie jestem szczęśliwy. There are no doubt subtle differences of style and emphasis between the two formulations, but the basic sense is the same. That is to say, the negative element nie may be said to have greater mobility within the sentence than the English un-, which is fixed, being always attached directly to another form.

This leads to a very basic distinction in linguistic analysis, namely the separation of free forms from those that are bound to others. Free forms may appear by themselves in various positions (though not by any means in any position whatsoever). They thus represent relatively independent elements, while bound forms on the other hand appear only in conjunction with others. They are thus strictly limited as to environment. In English, as it happens, the proportion of free forms is relatively high, that of bound forms relatively low. Some languages, like Chinese, have a still higher proportion of them; others a much lower (which is the same as to say, a higher proportion of bound forms).

---

[1] On the asterisk, see ch. 1, n. 2.

Let us take a pair of examples from the English language. Here we have a free form *like* which can appear in various positions. Sometimes it may be substituted (or translated into another language) by an expression meaning similar to; having the image of something else. Thus we say "He is very like his sister" or "Like whom did you say?" But at other times the same free form may be replaced by an expression meaning: to find something fitting or suitable (hence of the same image); hence pleasing and satisfactory. Examples of this free form are: "I like him" or "I began to like him" or "Like him? Of course not!" or "Like it or not, you must do it." There is also a bound form in English, namely an ending *-ly* which resembles *un-* insofar as it can never appear by itself and never in shifted position. It is a well-known suffix usually associated with words that we call adverbs, as in those like *happily, newly, noisily*. From the historical point of view *-ly* represents a shortened derivative form of the free form *like* (in the nominal sense) since both come from an Old English word *lic* meaning shape or substance or body. (Compare German *Leiche*.) Thus *happily* would mean, from the historical point of view, something like: in the shape or image of happiness. However, the modern speaker of English simply accepts the role of *-ly* as a bound form even in such neologisms as *cibernetically* or *nuclearly*, because he has become accustomed to it in the frequent use of more familiar words having the same termination.

Of course the borderline between free and bound forms is not entirely rigid. In English there is a word *strawberry* which may be separated into two elements, *straw+berry*. Here the first of the two appears also as a form existing independently in the word *straw* (related to the verb *strew*; the plant's runners would appear to have suggested the designation). The second element *-berry* is easily recognizable and is often used in a free form. But in words like *cranberry* or *whortleberry* (American *huckleberry*) the first elements are not movable and do not appear in varying contexts. Hence they are by nature bound.

Bound forms are thus associated with and in a sense subordinate to others. They have become traditionally classified under three categories: prefixes, suffixes and infixes, depending on whether they appear before, after, or in the midst of others. This does not mean, however, that a form bound in one context may not be free in another, nor that the central (associated) form is always itself free. The situation is complicated and can best be clarified by examples:

An instance of a bound prefix is the English *un-*, already mentioned. It should be stressed again, however, that in many languages, notably the Indo-European, there are prefixes which may also function as free forms. Thus in Latin the word *it* ("he goes") may receive the prefix *ex*, meaning out, out of. The result is *exit*, familiar as a loan-word in English. As such, it is indivisible. Both elements are bound. But in Latin *ex* also existed as a free form (a preposition), not only as a prefix. So also with English *outgoing*. On the other hand Polish *wyjść* meaning to go out has a prefix *wy-* corresponding to Latin *ex-* which is never found in that sense as a free form. It is always bound.

Bound forms appearing at the end of free forms are called suffixes. In the Indo-European languages such forms are less apt to have free counterparts than do prefixes. English has a few suffixes, not many, which show a dual function. Thus *heedless* with suffix *-less* means lacking heed, while the expression "six less [i.e. lacking] four" shows the form in free position, since other numbers could be substituted within the formula cited, giving "seven less one" and other expressions. Bound suffixes are very numerous in Indo-European languages. The Slavic languages, together with the Baltic and Indic, make extensive use of them; German manages with fewer; Dutch and English with still fewer. Thus in Polish if one wants to say "by means of an airplane" he will use the expression *samolotem*, where the bound suffix *-em*, incapable of free functioning, clearly conveys the sense of the expression "by means of." Other languages will use free forms like English *with* or *by*, and their equivalents. Usage varies widely in this respect.

Bound forms appearing in the midst of others are called infixes. In the Celtic languages special forms of personal pronouns—bound forms—are infixed between others, both free and bound. Thus in Old Welsh we have *neu-m-gorruc* equivalent to "now-has-me-made" with infixed -*me*-. Similarly (though for different historical reasons) the Spanish *conmigo* (literally "with-me-with"). There are verbal forms where the presence of a medial consonant may have a special significance, for instance Latin *fundō* "I pour" as opposed to *fūdī* "I have poured" or English *stand* as opposed to *stood*. These -*n*-'s are sometimes called infixes. One may perhaps compare these alterations of forms with the contrast to be found in such pairs of verbs in Polish as *wysiąść* with nasalized vowel (meaning to get out of a conveyance now, at once) and *wysiadać* with unnasalized vowel (meaning to get out of a conveyance any time, in general).

2. Some Special Problems Related to Bound Forms

So far we have discussed bound forms—prefixes, infixes and suffixes—which cluster about a central one. The central form is commonly called the root of a word. Sometimes it is easily recognizable as a potentially free form. Thus English *inflame*, when stripped of its prefix, yields the independent form *flame*; but the related word *inflammable*, when deprived of both prefix and suffix yields an element -*flam*- which does not exist independently. It is always bound. Yet it is sufficiently similar to *flame* to show a clear linguistic kinship. On the other hand it is less clear that the roots of English *im-pot-ent* and *im-poss-ible* are also related, though they are, -*poss*- being modified from -*pot*- having the general sense of power.

In other words, some roots are bound forms which may or may not be recognizable as related to other bound forms or to free ones; and they may or may not be self-explanatory. Again, some languages show the relationship more clearly than do others. In general it is usually clearest when the vocabulary of a language is relatively homogenous: that is, mostly made up of native elements. Polish for instance has a simple root form *brak* meaning lack or want and the like. It is easily recognizable in words like *za-brak-nąć* (meaning to fall short or be lacking in something) and *za-brak-ować* (meaning to reject something or throw it aside). Once the prefixes and suffixes of the verb forms are detached, we have got a self-explanatory root. And roots are sometimes recognizable even in modified forms. In Polish a root may be identified in a word like *ze-bra-nie*, meaning a meeting or gathering of people, but something like it is also to be found in *za-bier-ać*, meaning to take up or occupy, with its special form *za-br-ać* associated with it. Here we have a series of roots *-bra-*, *-bier-* and *-br-* which are obviously connected and can be related to the very general sense of carrying somethings (or some people) together. As a matter of fact, the root **b-r*, with or without intermediate vowel, is well known in a number of Indo-European languages. English *bear* (as verb) is but one example. On the other hand, relationships may not always be so clearly recognizable, as for instance in the case of *-pot-* with *-pos-* in words like English *impotent* and *impossible*, already cited; or English *vital* and *viable*, both derived from a Latin root *vit-* meaning life. Here the roots are alien to English and therefore not clearly recognizable. Yet in the light of historical studies the correlation may be established.

There is another problem connected with forms both free and bound, and that is the possibility of variations in their internal structure, which are independent of any association with other forms. For instance, in English there is a free form *sing* and beside it there exists another, namely *sang*, which is obviously a variant form of it, derived not by the addition of a suffix but by a change in the root vowel. This then is another possible way of indicating a modification in the use and function of a given form. Internal modification of the vowel may seem to resemble the use of an infix, already discussed, but it is actually a quite separate process.

It may be wondered, by the way, why we should say that *sing* is the primary form and *sang* is derived from it, rather than the reverse. In the same way one might ask why Polish *miał* is regarded as being derived from *mieć* instead of vice versa. There is to be sure a certain element of convention, which at times may appear arbitrary, in the manner of presenting such relationships as we find them in the grammars of a language. Yet there are reasons why the traditional presentation is usually justifiable. To explain them would require an excursion into various fields such as historical linguistics, syntactic structure and even the psychology of language. But it may be indicated at least why, for instance, it is the so-called first case (nominative) of a noun that is entered in a dictionary as the primary form: Polish *kobieta* rather than *kobiety*, Latin *fēmina* rather than *fēminae*, English *woman* rather than *woman's*. Historically, the practice is largely due to imitation of ancient Greek usage, but the justification lies in the fact that the noun appearing in the first case will often determine other forms in a sentence (notably verbal forms) rather than being determined by them. It is relatively freely chosen, while the choice of other cases is more restricted by surrounding elements in the sentence. As for the sequence in which other cases are presented, this is much more a matter of arbitrary convention.

An orderly presentation of all the modified forms of a word involving its relation to other words in a sentence is called its inflexion. In the Indo-European languages, inflexion is mostly realized by suffixing a special set of bound forms and by internal change as in the instances just discussed. Prefixes are less often used. It should be emphasized that bound forms constitute inflexional endings only when they serve exclusively to indicate relationship to other words in a sentence, whether determining their forms or being determined by them. Thus the prefix *un-* in *unhappy* is not regarded as a grammatical inflexion, since both adjectives, the positive and the negative, can have identical positions in a sentence and stand in identical relation to other words appearing in it. The absence of any inflexional ending at all is sometimes highly significant. Thus in the Polish word *kobiet* the lack of a suffix tells us very much about the way the form may appear in a sentence and the relation it will have to other words in it. When comparing such a form with others in the same inflexion it is convenient to say that it has a zero suffix.

3. Morphology and what It Means

The study of free and bound forms, their modifications and relations to one another in a specific language has traditionally been called morphology. In this sense the term has in practice been limited to the study of inflexions. Morphology comes from the Greek word μορφή (*morphḗ*) meaning any kind of shape or form, corresponding to the very general sense in which we have been speaking of free and bound forms. Thus morphology might well be expected to include the study of all the relations possible among both kinds of forms, not only the relations of inflexional affixes to roots.

Theoretically it should be possible to make a complete inventory of all the identifiable forms, free and bound, in any language. In practice as we have seen it is not really easy to separate identifiable from non-identifiable forms. There are many borderline cases. Still, let us assume the possibility for the moment. The result would be a dictionary listing separately each identifiable form such as English *sing, flame, un-, -ing, -able* and Polish *mieć, brak, -li, -ować* and *-owi*. It would also include English *-ed* and *-t*, as two different bound forms used to express the past tense of certain verbs: compare *wait-ed* with *pas-t* (related to *pass*; it is spelled *passed* as a verb form but here also pronounced *past*). And it would include Polish *-i* as well as *-y* as two different bound forms used to express the plural number of certain nouns: compare *dom-y* with *domk-i*. We may call each of these recognizable forms, bound and un-bound, a morph. The word has been coined in recent times by linguists in order to designate all kinds of free and bound forms in all positions, each time they appear.

But a moment's thought will show that the inventory could be reduced and simplified if we take into account the minor variations due to environment. In English the morph *-ed* appearing in the verb *waited* will also be found attached to other roots ending in consonants like *-t* or *-d*, enunciated on the teeth; the morph *-d* (spelled *-ed* also) will be found attached to roots ending in a voiced consonant like *-z*, for instance *gaze-d*; while the morph *-t* will appear after another type of consonant, as in *pas-t*. In Polish, the morph *-y* appearing on the noun *dom-y* appears also in many other nouns, but when the root ends in *-k* or *-g*, the morph will be *-i*, for reasons connected with the Polish system of articulation. In such cases we may say that Polish *i-* and *-y* are allomorphs or variations of the same form depending only on environment; their functions are identical. (The prefix *allo-* is taken from the Greek, meaning other.) Similarly with the variously pronounced endings for the past tense of certain English verbs such as *wait*, *gaze*, *pass*.

If we group together a set of obviously related allomorphs, varying only because of their articulatory environment but having otherwise the same function, we may call each set a morpheme. This word is also a creation of modern linguistic science. It subsumes all the allomorphs of one morph into a single entity. For instance, Polish *-y* and *-i* as nominal endings really represent only one morpheme. But since *-y* appears statistically more frequently than *-i* (the latter being limited to positions following *k* and *g*, as in *leki*, *drogi*), we assume that the morph *-y* is fundamental, while *-i* is a more strictly conditioned allomorph. Together *-i* and *-y* are thus one morpheme. Each time either one is actually spoken it is realized as a morph.

It is possible to have homonymous morphemes in a language. The same form, free or bound, may appear in such differing environments as to indicate that it has two or more differing, often even contrasting functions. In English, for instance, the free forms *see* and *sea* are identical in pronunciation, but they are seldom confused in a conversation because they usually occupy different positions in a sentence: for instance "I see the sea." Yet ambiguity may arise in some situations. As it happens, English possesses a third form homonymous with the other two (spelled *see*) which comes ultimately from Latin *sēde(s)* meaning a seat. Today the word is rather archaic and limited in usage. It refers to the throne or official seat of a bishop. Still we may imagine a situation in which there could be doubt whether a speaker was referring to a body of water (*sea*) or a throne (*see*), since these morphemes are homonyms. And a comparable confusion may arise because of homonymous bound forms. Latin had a prefix *in-* (with allomorph *im-*) which really represented two morphemes. In certain contexts, *in-* carried the meaning of in or into; in others it served as a negative. The former appears in the English loan-word *inflammable* ("flaming into," hence easily set afire), while the latter appears in another loan-word *inflexible* (that is, not flexible, not capable of being bent). Here the ambiguity could have serious consequences. Certain cleaning fluids known to be dangerously prone to ignite were formerly labelled with the warning expression "Inflammable!" But housekeepers not conversant with the origin of the word, and misled by the homonymous prefixes, interpreted it to mean "not at all flammable." The result was often a serious explosion in the kitchen. Consequently it became desirable to use a different warning on the bottles, something like "Danger! Easily flammable."

At times the consequences of misinterpreting homonymous morphemes are comic rather than disastrous. Once again an English example will serve. The morpheme *sex* exists as a free form and also as a bound one. When free, it can only refer to a matter of biological distinction between male and female (Latin *sexus*). When bound, it may have the same reference as in the word *sexual*, but may likewise stand for the number six (Latin *sex*) as in words like *sex-partite* or *sex-tant*. Confusion between the homonymous morphemes has led some uninstructed speakers of English in the United States to conclude that the word *sextette* (that is a musical composition requiring six voices or six instruments) had something to do with *sex* in the biological sense. Hence they have interpreted the announcement of performance by a musical sextette as the promise of a very decadent type of visual entertainment.

Apart from confusion caused by homonyms, it may be said that the frequency of appearance of a morpheme is directly related to the readiness with which it will be comprehended. If it is rare it is less likely to be understood than if it is commonly used. Archaic forms and those borrowed from foreign languages naturally fall into the former category. English possesses an archaic variant form of *like* (discussed in section 1), namely *lich*, in the special sense of a corpse or dead body. The essential connexion with *like* in the sense of "having the same image" is clear on a moment's reflexion. However, when the average nonphilological speaker of English refers to the lichgate in a churchyard, where a corpse may be rested on the way to burial, he is only dimly aware, if at all, of the significance of the morpheme *lich-*. A borrowed word, especially one of limited currency, may be modified in common speech so that its unfamiliar elements are made to resemble better-known morphemes. The medical term *arthr-itis*, of Greek origin, contains a second element which is a fairly familiar suffix appearing in words like *appendicitis, meningitis* and the like. It has come to have the sense of inflammation or disease of a certain part of the body. The first element is however less familiar. It comes from the Greek *arthron*, meaning joint. In popular pronunciation however the word is sometimes distorted to *arthur-itis*, as if the disease afflicted only persons having the name Arthur. Similarly the borrowed name of the vegetable *asparagus* (Polish *szparag*, both from Greek *asparagos*) has been transformed in colloquial speech into *sparrowgrass* though it has no relation, historical or otherwise, with sparrows or grass. French colonists in the New World, probably discouraged by the vigorous conditions they found there, named a place of settlement Purgatoire; the name exists today transformed in English as Picket-wire.

Such transformation of strange or alien elements into familiar morphemes is known as popular etymology. The term is not very satisfactory, since the process does not really represent etymology in the sense of analysis based on the historical origin of words. However, it is current among specialists and may well stand.

One final point should be made in connexion with morphemes. Some of them not only appear more often than others at a given time in the history of a language, but some are also more often used than others in creating new words—neologisms—which may or may not be accepted in time as part of the current vocabulary. A morpheme capable of giving rise to new words is said to be productive; others, though identifiable, are unproductive. The English suffix *-able* (derived from the Latin) having the sense of something capable of or adapted to a specific activity, has been employed in our times to create the term *fissionable*, applied in modern physics to those types of atomic nuclei which are capable of fission (split-

ting), thus causing the release of enormous quantities of energy
(e.g. the splitting of uranium nuclei). Though recently coined, the
term is clear because its parts are clear. There are many examples
of such active morphemes in English as also in other languages:
compare the *z-* with its allomorph *s-* which appears in Polish words
like *z-irytować* and *s-paraliżować*. Here a native morpheme has
been adapted in recent times to a foreign loan-word and it is still
active. But in a word like German *Ant-wort* the first element does
not serve to create new linguistic forms. At one time *ant-* with its
allomorphs such as *and-* and *an-*, all of them implying a sense of
opposition or response, was active in the Germanic languages.
A trace of the old initial morpheme may be detected in the English
answer, although the word today functions as a single morpheme,
quite indivisible. In earlier times, before 1066, the word was
andswaru, in which two separate morphemes were clearly recognizable (the second being connected with modern English *swear*).
The prefix *and-* could then be found in a considerable number of
other words, but it has long since ceased to be productive.

4. FUSED FORMS AND ETYMOLOGY

A word like *answer* may be regarded as the result of the fusion
of two morphemes into one. Only in the light of historical studies
is the process revealed, and such studies are possible, of course,
only on the basis of early written sources. The farther back these
go, the more we can learn about the way morphemes are related
to one another and how they have been transformed throughout
history. It is sometimes possible to get a view of relationships being
so fundamentally transformed that they affect the entire structure
of a language. Early free forms may be merely juxtaposed, later
on combined more or less loosely (by agglutination) and still
later subordinated to others or even fused completely.

The study of linguistic elements as they appear at a given period,
without regard to their historical background, is said to be synchronic. On the other hand a study which concerns itself with
these elements as they have developed over the course of centuries

is called diachronic. The diachronic study of words and the morphemes that enter into them, setting aside inflexional endings, is known as etymology. Where sufficient written records of a language exist, extending over a considerable span of time, it is possible to compile an etymological dictionary showing earlier forms with appropriate definitions deduced from usage in contexts. Such materials will often reveal changes not only in forms but in meaning. The shifts in usage sometimes throw very interesting light on the way people of an earlier age envisaged themselves in relation to the universe and one another. A slight modification in the form of a word may be accompanied by a great shift in its meaning, and vice versa. This leads us to the entire problem of historical semantics, which will be discussed in the next chapter. At present, one point should be stressed. Beginners in the historical study of any language sometimes get the impression that an earlier form of a word somehow discloses its "real" meaning, and that a later form, including the present one, must somehow represent a distortion. Before the rise of modern linguistic science, change of any sort was looked upon as corruption, perhaps under the influence of the Biblical account of Adam's giving names to the birds and beasts. A vocabulary created in Eden was assumed to be perfect; therefore all changes had to be for the worse, beginning with the confusion of tongues at the Tower of Babel.

Today we look at the phenomenon of linguistic change in a different way. We do not pass value judgements on the morphology of one period as compared to that of another. The form and use or meaning of a word (or its parts) in current speech are right for today. If etymological research shows a different form and use of that same word 1000 years ago, we assume that they were right for their time too. In each historical situation, taken separately, we adopt the synchronic point of view. But when we compare the two situations we must perforce adopt the diachronic point of view.

A few simple examples will suffice. German has an adjective *elend*, meaning miserable or wretched. An etymological dictionary will tell us that *elend* is derived from an expression *eli-lendi* literally meaning in an alien land; banished. Curiously enough, English *wretched* also comes from a term applied to an exile. Among the early Germanic peoples, a sense of solidarity, of belonging to a tribe and serving a chieftain, must have been very strong. We know this from poems expressing the deep sorrow of wandering exiles separated from their homes and kinsmen. But today *elend* is a completely fused form and its application has been widened greatly. It designates much more than an exile's misery—partly because modern society is different from early Germanic. Emigration need not be a tragic affair in our times.

Another example may be cited from English. There is a verb *atone* (pronounced *a-'tōn*) meaning to reconcile; the derivative noun is *atonement*, or the act of reconciliation. Historically the verb arose from a combination of *at* plus *one*, meaning in general simply to set at one; but accentuation has caused fusion and obscured the relationship of two morphemes originally distinct. Today therefore the verb functions as a single morpheme and its application has become restricted. Whereas the morpheme sequence "at one" (two free forms) can be interrupted, as in the sentence "I came at just one o'clock," the fused form *atone* is indivisible. Besides, *atone* has become greatly restricted in usage, being now primarily associated with theology and ethics (one makes atonement for an injury inflicted). The process of fusion is as complete as with German *elend*. In any event the contemporary usage is the one of primary interest to contemporary speakers of English, studying the language from the synchronic point of view·

One final example. German has an adjective *traur-ig*, cognate with English *drear-y*, both meaning sad or depressing. It is interesting to know that both are derived from a root with the meaning to drip with blood, to bleed, as for instance in the Old Icelandic verb *dreyr-a*. The earlier associations were with fighting and killing, exploits conspicuous in the lives of early Germanic warriors. Today the two related adjectives refer to subjective moods rather than objective actions. The diachronic shift is interesting for the investigator of social history as well as the linguist. But it would be a mistake to assume that the older meaning is the "real" one and the modern one is somehow subordinate to it. Each one is equally valid for the period to which it belongs.

The procedure for historical study is simply this. One collects all instances of the cognate forms at an early stage of the related languages concerned; one compares their contexts and usages and in this way establishes the synchronic meaning common to all. Then one collects instances of the same cognate forms as they appear at a later period — say a thousand years later — and establishes a second synchronic meaning. A diachronic comparison will reveal the shifts that have occurred. A knowledge of external factors (social and political history, technology, etc.) will often elucidate the reasons for the changes and then deepen our understanding of their operation. But the fundamental method is the comparison of one synchronic description with another, without preference for one above another.

5. WHAT IS A WORD?

So far the word *word* has been rather loosely employed as if it were self-explanatory; yet we have seen (in section 2) that the boundary between free forms (words) and bound forms (non-words) is by no means always clear. In writing and printing, some languages make use of a convention of spacing between free forms, but the practice is not universally followed. In ancient Sanskrit, for instance, whole utterances corresponding to what we call sentences were written down without a break. If you listen to people speaking a language quite foreign to you, you will be aware of certain pauses marking off sections of the discourse, but between those pauses you will not be able at first to identify the smaller units, whether free or bound. And if you are investigating a language which has never been written down because its speakers lack an alphabet, you will have to make use of various devices to identify those free forms which may appear separately in different contexts. This will be easier in some cases than others. One factor which may cause difficulty is the tendency to have the final sound of one word modified because of the initial sound of the next, or the reverse. The boundary between the two is thus obscured, as it was for instance in Sanskrit and the ancient Celtic languages.

However, there are certain formal tests which are helpful in identifying words. The task is easiest where the language makes use for the most part of short free forms placed in juxtaposition without use of subordinate bound forms such as inflexional endings (for instance, various dialects of Chinese). In inflected languages, which present a more complicated problem, accentuation may be a guide. Thus in Polish the incidence of stress on the next-to-the-last (penultimate) syllable of words helps to mark off their boundaries. (This is not an infallible guide, however. The principle also operates with words closely related in a spoken sentence, as for instance in the expression *ná wsi*.) In Icelandic and Finnish, accent always falls on the first syllable. Vowel harmony is a guide to a greater or lesser extent in the Finno-Ugric languages insofar as they reflect the general principle that the kind of vowel appearing in the first syllable of a word will determine what vowels may appear in the next syllables, down to the boundary with the next word. In English the situation is less clear but in certain cases accent does help us to decide whether a sequence of two morphemes such as *black+board* is to be treated as one word or two, and also to distinguish between *nitrate* (one word) and *night rate* (two words). In some languages moreover the final sound of a word may be subject to special modifications which help to signal its boundary. Thus the genitive plural of Polish *lada* (meaning a chest or box), namely *lad*, will be pronounced with a final *-t* instead of *-d* as similarly the German word *Hand* is pronounced *Hant*. Such tests of accent and pronunciation cannot be applied in all languages, but where they do apply they offer at least some guidance in the demarcation of words.

Another technique may be helpful in identifying separate words in a strange language, namely the use of formulas of speech or frame sentences. The learner may say "This is a..." (Polish—*To jest...*) followed by various free forms such as *pen, book, house* (*pióro, książka, dom*) and if he is understood he will assume that he has in each case employed a recognizable word of the language concerned. But he may be misled by some of the unclear or ambiguous combinations already mentioned. He may find that the following three requests will evoke active responses on the part of a native speaker of English indicating that they have been understood as comprehensible, being made up of normal words:

> Give me a straw;
> Give me a berry;
> Give me a strawberry.

But if a request is made "Give me a *cran*" (instead of *cranberry*) the response will probably be, "What did you say? What do you want?" The native speaker's failure to understand has indicated that *cran-* is a non-word.

Pauses in spoken discourse occur normally after groups of words run together, not after single ones. Only in response to such a request as "Repeat that, please! I didn't understand you" will a speaker tend to enunciate each word separately with pedantic slowness. This will of course help the listener. When words are run together without pauses, they are said to be in closed juncture. When pauses occur, there is said to be terminal juncture after the last word. When a word is final—that is, followed by silence instead of a mere slight pause—it may be marked by a special kind of intonation or speech melody peculiar to this kind of terminal juncture. But the intonation will not always be an aid in showing the initial boundary of the final word.

There are languages in which an entire statement assumes the form of what we would call a single word, made up of interdependent bound and unbound forms. All of this goes to show how difficult it is to make a universal definition of the term word, applicable to all languages.

A convenient dictionary definition of a word is "the smallest unit of speech that has meaning when taken by itself." Yet the phrase "when taken by itself" is not entirely clear. For instance, in English the morpheme *anti-*, taken from the Greek, is usually bound, hence is a non-word, as in *anti-aircraft, anti-body, anti-toxin* and the like. Nevertheless *anti* may appear as a free form, that is to say as a separate word. In reply to the question "What is his attitude to the new plan?" a perfectly acceptable and understandable answer in colloquial language might be, "Oh, he's very anti," i.e., opposed. Here a unit of speech normally not taken by itself is detached and yet understood. Hence it must have meaning, even in isolation. Another possible answer to the question might have been, "Oh, he's very pro," i.e., favourable. Again, an instance of a bound form understood in isolation. Once more we observe the lack of a sharp boundary between linguistic categories.

Another term in the definition just quoted presents even greater difficulties, namely meaning. The problem of definition arises in connexion with both morpheme and word. If a word can be made up of a single morpheme, then morphemes also must have meaning. In fact, a commonly accepted definition for morpheme is a linguistic unit that cannot be subdivided into smaller, meaningful parts. In other words, it is a minimal linguistic unit possessing meaning.

But what is meaning? A naive response to the question might be "meaning is the definition you find in a dictionary" or "the meaning of a form like *anti-* or *pro-* or *plan* is the explanation I give when someone asks me what it means." But a moment's reflection will indicate that the problem of explaining the meaning of linguistic forms has very serious philosophical implications.

Each person, speaking of himself and his own experience with words, will tend to use expressions like "As I understand it" or "For me it's a pleasant (or unpleasant) term," or "I always thought it meant so-and-so." He speaks subjectively from his own point of view on the basis of remembered experience recorded in his persisting consciousness or memory. But each person's consciousness at any given moment is private and individual. No two human beings have ever had the same experiences or the same abilities in using and interpreting them. In this sense each person is alien to all others. Is it possible therefore for any two human beings to establish a contact of consciousness? Can one human being ever be sure that another has consciousness at all? He cannot himself penetrate into it. All he can do is observe the behaviour of another person and interpret it in the light of what he calls his own consciousness.

This well-known human situation has given rise to several philosophical interpretations which are important for linguistics. Those who concentrate their attention on the barriers between one human consciousness and another may decide to study and record external behaviour alone. We can never reach or share in another's memories and subjective experiences, they say; these are inaccessible and therefore for scientific purposes they do not exist. Consciousness can be eliminated as a factor in linguistic description. Instead we shall concentrate exclusively on the stimuli offered by language and the responses evoked by it, especially linguistic responses (though gesture may also be taken into consideration). Such scholars are called behaviourists or linguistic mechanists pure and simple, since they envisage the situation of two people talking as something like an interchange between two machines. All that is pertinent for scientific description (they say) is the series of stimuli and responses between the two. Other scholars, while agreeing that observable phenomena in such a specific situation ought to be carefully recorded, without any appeal to consciousness, nevertheless insist that language is not to be understood only as it is realized in isolated dialogues (comparable to the simple stimulus-and-response situation of Pavlov's famous dogs) but must be seen as a complex social phenomenon involving many speakers in a community. The intricacies of human (as opposed to animal) communications require an especially elaborate description, taking into account many factors of social environment — but still dispensing with the postulate of consciousness. This is the approach of the social behaviourists. Marxist materialists recognize consciousness as a special function of matter and they do not exclude it from discussions of language. Finally, linguistic idealists may be said to emphasize subjective factors at the expense of others, but at the same time they have interested themselves in both the psychological aspects of language and its relation to human culture.

Returning to the specific problem of morphemes, we may say that their relation to meaning has been handled differently, as is to be expected, by adherents of different philosophical schools. Morphemes have been defined by some writers in terms of their frequency, mobility and distribution in the flow of speech without any reference whatever to meaning. Other writers admit the test of meaning but define this in terms of linguistic environment only; still others admit the relevance of social environment as well, but avoid any appeal to subjective factors in a speech situation: that is, to what they would regard as the inaccessible consciousness of an interlocutor.

This is not the place to enter into the age-long debate about the existence, or rather the pertinence of human consciousness for scientific descriptions of human behaviour. Each individual person may report that something happens to him privately between the time that he hears a set of morphemes and the moment when he makes a reply: memories may have been evoked, some silent deliberation may have occurred, and so on. But it is true that this inner history can never be directly known to an outsider. To this extent the mechanistic behaviourists present the situation correctly, but there is evidence which leads to an acceptance of the hypothesis of consciousness possessed by other persons than oneself. (Similarly we accept the hypothesis of electric currents running through wires, although we experience only results from them such as shocks, fluctuations in instruments of measurement like ammetres, etc.) For one thing, sociological studies of such complex phenomena as political propaganda, advertizing, literary fashions and the like would seem to indicate that a process of interpretation intervenes between reception of written or spoken stimuli and the response to them. If a listener has fallen asleep or fainted before his radio, he may be said to have lost his consciousness of it. If he is awake he may react in very many ways, depending on the extent of his agreement or disagreement with what was said. At the moment he may not react at all; but there is evidence that his behaviour at a later time will be affected by what he heard, that is to say by memory plus personal interpretation, plus shared social experiences. These factors point to the existence of an element in the situation which it is convenient to call his consciousness.

For linguists the philosophical problem is of interest chiefly as it involves questions of methodology. Investigators of unrecorded alien languages soon discovered that they could not rely on the simple technique of asking a native speaker "What do you mean by that?" The informant's explanation might be naive and misleading, or incomprehensible to the questioner. Hence there arose an understandable distrust of explanations based on meaning, and a recourse to purely objective tests such as distribution and frequency and morphemic environment.

But these objective tests may at times be extremely cumbersome, even wasteful. Let us say, for instance, that the distribution of the ambiguous *in-* prefix in English words such as *inflammable* and *insupportable* has caused serious burns on the part of naive users of certain fluids. One could warn those users to take account of the frequency of occurrences and linguistic environments of the morpheme *in-*, but in ordinary usage it is better to appeal to their assumed consciousness and simply explain the two "meanings" of *in-* in order to avoid accidents. Similarly, it has been pointed out that in an ambiguous sequence of morphemes the appeals to distribution and the like may take more time and energy than appeals to extra-linguistic knowledge. In English, for instance, the reply to a question "What did you say he's doing?" may be "He's lying." Under certain conditions this might mean "He is telling a lie; not the truth," and in others it might mean "He is reclining; not standing up." Here the extra-linguistic environment is obviously important in determining the interpretation of the word *lying*. Frequency and distribution will not offer decisive help, since "He's lying" can appear in identical linguistic contexts yet evoke divergent non-linguistic responses. Such ambiguous utterances have been cited by critics of the strictly mechanistic school. One of them is the sentence "She made him a good husband because she made him a good wife." By elaborate methods of substitution it might be possible to show that this sequence of morphemes *she-made-him* performs two different functions in the two parts of the utterance;

but it seems easier to rely on the extra-linguistic knowledge that women are not husbands and men are not wives. Here again reference to meaning as commonly understood (implying consciousness on the listener's part) appears to simplify the task of explanation. And simplicity is desirable in scientific description, provided of course that it does not become misleading.

In discussing words and their histories in the next chapter, therefore, we shall make use of the term "meaning" without further apology or explanation. For some readers it will imply only objective factors, sometimes requiring elaborate description. For others it will imply both objective and subjective factors. The latter may be admitted to be conjectural from the mechanistic point of view, but the assumption of their existence somewhat facilitates the task of description. It is mainly for this reason that the postulate of consciousness will also be admitted in ensuing discussions. If nothing else, this postulate permits a shortcut in telling about the multiple, complex and diversified ways in which various individuals of a given speech community have responded to morpheme stimuli throughout the ages.

CHAPTER 4

WORDS AND THEIR MEANINGS: SEMANTICS

1. THE CONVENTIONAL NATURE OF LINGUISTIC SIGNS

From all that has been said so far it must be clear that the words of any language are almost all of them arbitrary. There is no intrinsic relation, let us say, between words such as *Buch, book, książka, livre* and *книга* on the one hand and the object that one takes into one's hands to read. Yet linguistic habit establishes such a relation within specific languages. To be sure, there are words in all languages which are imitative of sounds in nature (English *hiss* and *buzz*; Polish *syczeć* and *bzykać*) and therefore these must be classified as non-arbitrary. However, they are relatively few in number. We shall for practical purposes ignore them in the present discussion.

Having indicated that a word is to be understood formally as a linguistic entity composed of one or more morphemes, we now ask ourselves: how do words function as a means of communication among people speaking the same language, and what is their relation to the world of things and events outside of language?

As point of departure it will be useful to define a word as a linguistic sign (*signum*). A sign in general is any observed phenomenon which points to another, as when we say that clouds are a sign that rain is coming, or a red light at a traffic crossing is a sign that a driver will get into trouble if he moves his car in the direction thus marked. When a sign is invested with multiple complex associations, extending beyond the rather simple correlations here exemplified, it may be said to become a symbol. Thus the colour red may in certain wider situations—not just at street-crossings—point to broad political action today, or evoke memories of historical events which occurred in 1848, 1871, 1917. Or again, the simple sign of a pictured apple may under certain conditions suggest not only a specific fruit but (as in medieval art) the Christian dogma of the Fall of Man, the loss of innocence in the Garden of Eden. It is the same with words as linguistic signs: they may have relatively clear or relatively complex (symbolic) functions, but they are all signs.

And now comes the question: To what do they point? On the surface this seems like a simple question indeed. The linguistic sign (or word) *apple* points primarily to the known fruit existing in the objective material world. Here one is tempted to assert that the fruit itself can be identified with the meaning of the linguistic sign. But can it? In the first place that would be the same as saying that one eats the meaning of the word *apple* when one eats the fruit: a clear absurdity. In the second place, there are very many linguistic signs which cannot be simply and unambiguously related to objects and events in the world of nature. Such for instance are words like English *from*, Polish *od*, German *von*, French *de*. Again we are reminded of the essentially conventional nature of linguistic signs, and also of their wide range. Not all by any means are names of things.

Such being the situation, it is understandable that more than one explanation has been suggested for the relationship of linguistic signs to their meaning (however that term is understood). Curiously enough, linguists were slow in turning their attention to the problem. It was not until the end of the 19th century that the area known as semantics was recognized as part of linguistic science and subjected to initial exploration. An outstanding founder of contemporary linguistics, Ferdinand de Saussure, decided to call the specifically linguistic sign a *signifiant* (that is to say, a signifier), and the thing to which it refers—the *signifié* (i.e., that which is signified). By the latter term, de Saussure insisted, we must understand — not objective phenomena in the world of nature, but the "concept" in the listener's mind. This would mean the remembered experiences of speech-situations which enable him to interpret the linguistic sign and react to it appropriately, whether at the moment of hearing (reading) it or at a later time. The role of the *signifié* (a purely subjective factor) is to be studied in terms of the here and now, not the past: synchronically, therefore, for any given period of history. The fact that in German *das Buch* once meant the wood of a beech-tree means nothing to the average speaker of German today; it does not affect his subjective associations with the word. If at an earlier period speakers of German attached a signification (concept) of a kind of tree to the same linguistic sign, that fact should likewise be recorded as a phenomenon of synchronic analysis valid for the previous epoch but now irrelevant. Presumably one could work out a causal relationship between the two recorded facts, resulting in a synthesis of the two types of description, synchronic and diachronic. (See ch. 3, sec. 5.) But de Saussure did not live, unfortunately, to develop the many stimulating suggestions contained in the course of his lectures, edited and printed after his death. Hence we do not know how he might have proposed to bridge the gap between one synchronic description and another. In the case of *das Buch*, for instance, it would be necessary to investigate recorded usages of the expression in contexts covering a number of centuries, and thus determine when the modern application of the term arose. For complete understanding of the shift it would be desirable to turn to extralinguistic knowledge such as the history of human technology. From this we learn that the early Germanic peoples scratched their alphabets (called runic) on hard substances such as stone, iron or wood. In fact, the basic meaning of English *write* was at one time to scratch, to cut. The wood of the beech tree (*die Buche*) must have been used for this purpose.

The account of meaning given by de Saussure implies a three-cornered situation in which only two elements are of interest to the linguist. It may be represented thus:

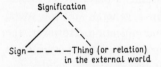

The solid line represents the sole relationship pertinent for linguists; the dotted lines represent irrelevant relationships.

Certain writers following after de Saussure have adopted and somewhat modified his picture of the situation. A well-known study by two English writers, C. K. Ogden and I. A. Richards, offers the following scheme:

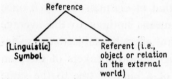

Here the term symbol corresponds to de Saussure's linguistic sign, reference corresponds to de Saussure's "concept" or signification, and referent corresponds to something in the external world. But the diagram of Ogden and Richards admits of a pertinent relationship between reference and referent, which was denied by de Saussure.

The triangular situation presented by de Saussure, Ogden and Richards may be compared with the linear situation presented by the American linguist Leonard Bloomfield. The latter's description is concerned with external factors only, thus:

$$S \to s \to r \to R$$

where S and R stand for non-linguistic stimuli and responses respectively, and s and r for linguistic ones. Thus S might be the sight of an apple, s the spoken words "Give it to me," r the reply "Here it is" and R the gesture of handing over the apple. There is no place assigned here to the role played by subjective factors, which are apparently regarded as quite irrelevant for scientific linguistic description. Although Bloomfield's scheme has been elaborated and explained in much subtle detail by his followers (for instance, Eugene Nida), it remains basic for the school associated with his name.

In a sense it may be said that all three schemes just reproduced have an element of artificiality about them. They are over-simplified because all of them concentrate on individual linguistic situations involving individual speakers and listeners at a given moment of time. To be sure, the terms signification and reference imply past accumulated experience on the listener's part. Moreover, all the authorities mentioned recognize in a general way the social nature of language as a means of communication. However, the complex social environment of speaking (the creation of utterances) is not and in fact cannot be adequately represented in the diagrams suggested—or in fact in any diagrams.

It is worth noting that structuralists have defined the unit of meaning attached to a morpheme as a sememe, and have provided the term episememe for the meaning of a grammatical construction (see ch. 6, sec. 4). Each separately definable meaning attached to a morpheme is to be called a seme, just as each individual variant of a phoneme is a phone. (With semes, however, there is a special problem of homonymity, as we have observed in the English prefix *in-* which may signify both a positive intensive and a negative seme.) Other terms proposed are: macrosememe for the meaning of an idiom, ethnosememe for a meaning whose referent involves the non-linguistic aspects of a situation, etc.[1] At this point, however, the terminology threatens to become hampering rather than helpful. One may well ask: Is there any referent which does not involve non-linguistic aspects of a situation? And how shall we number the ethnosemes which may be said to cluster about a given referent?

2. THE SOCIETAL ENVIRONMENT OF WORDS

Obviously, the give-and-take of acoustic linguistic signs in a conversation between two people presupposes a communal agreement as to how they are to be interpreted. This agreement rests on many complex factors. It assumes a vast number of experiences shared by all members of a speech community in a generally similar way. At the same time it is not a fixed or rigid sort of agreement, for it is subject to change in the course of time. At any given period, however, there must be a general consensus of opinion about the interpretation (meaning, reference) of words within the community, else no two persons could achieve mutual comprehensibility. (See ch. 3, sec. 5.)

The social environment determining the use of words was stressed by one of the earliest pioneers in the field of semantics, Michel Bréal. In his *Essai de Sémantique* (1897) Bréal spoke of differentiations of usage and choice of words depending on class distinctions. He cited the fact that in the language of Cambodia

---

[1] See J. Greenberg, "Concerning Inferences from Linguistic to Nonlinguistic Data," *Language in Culture*, ed. Harry Hoijer (University of Chicago Press, 1954), pp. 3–19.

quite different words are used to refer to the simple act of eating, depending on whether the person involved is a king, a chief, or an ordinary person. This may seem strange to us, but an analogy will readily be found in the use of equivalents for the second personal pronoun in several contemporary European languages. German has its gradation of *Sie, Ihr,* and *Du,* depending on degrees of intimacy and also social relationship; Polish is even more complicated in its hierarchy of pronominal expressions ranging from *Pan/Pani* (literally: "the lord, the lady" in the sense of "you") and *Państwo* (a neuter form used in referring to both "lords" and "ladies"), to *wy* and *ty* (plural and singular) used in less formal social situations. Russian is, like French, relatively simple in distinguishing gradations of social relationship (*вы* versus *ты*, *vous* versus *tu*), but English is still simpler: it has but one word, *you*, to refer to all persons addressed, whether singular or plural. This too has social implications.

Here we have examples of semantic usage dependent on extra-linguistic factors, namely the way in which individuals envisage their social relations with one another. It may be said that until recent times too little attention has been devoted to the interrelationship of the social environment with linguistic practice. Early interest in semantics concentrated on the etymologies of individual words where changes of meanings could be historically traced. However, interesting studies have been undertaken during recent decades in the border territory where language and social history overlap.

Over thirty years ago, a German scholar, Jost Trier, suggested that words should be grouped together according to the fields of human interest and activity which they represent (*Bedeutungs-felder*). Investigation of meanings should concentrate first of all on the interrelationships of terms appearing within a given group at a given historical period. That is to say, the initial description should be synchronic. But a second synchronic description of the same terms and their equivalents may be made for a later period, and then it will be proper to inquire what shifts of meaning have recurred in the interim. By a series of leaps, then, Trier undertakes to combine synchronic and diachronic analysis in semantics. He also undertakes to correlate the changes in meaning with changes in the world of culture in general.

These attempts by Trier seemed at the time very promising, and they inspired a number of studies along the lines he had suggested. Research in semantic fields can be facilitated by the existence of thesauruses and technical dictionaries in various languages. But the materials used by Trier himself were limited. He confined himself to an investigation of the medieval German vocabulary (nouns only) referring to the field of intellectual activity. So did some of his followers. It may be said that although Trier announced a very desirable program of semantic analysis in the light of social environment, its execution remained inadequate. Later writers have supplemented and corrected Trier's work in many ways. Porzig, for instance, in his book *Das Wunder der Sprache* (1950) has extended the range of vocabulary in a specific field to include verbs and adjectives as well as nouns; he also introduced the valuable relationship of semantic implication: to walk implies feet, to grasp implies hands, etc. But these suggestions are not fully developed. The social environment is but vaguely referred to.— In general it may be said that the critics (both Eastern and Western) of the *Feldtheorie* of Trier and his school are well justified. The application of the theory requires very extensive and detailed knowledge, not only of linguistics but also of social history. We have yet to see a fully developed cooperation between these two disciplines.

At present one can but suggest how semantic field studies may be better pursued than in the past. It might be desirable, for instance, to begin with groups of words having reference to phenomena more readily defined in objective terms than those relating to intellectual activity. The honorific terminology of a ruling class or dominant clique in one period may be compared with that of another with instructive results if social history is properly taken into account. It has been pointed out that medieval words connected with chivalry (German *Ritter*, Polish *rycerz*, Russian *рыцарь*, French *chevalier* and its cognates such as Spanish *caballero*) all evoke the image of a man on a horse as symbol of authority. This has something to do with the nature of feudalism and its social foundation in small communities often engaged in equestrian warfare with one another. It might be instructive to make a study of groups of words related to authority in modern times. Many of them are simply archaisms. For instance, the American term *senator* was simply taken over from ancient Roman usage where it meant one of an assemblage of old men. In Rome it was age which suggested authority, as is and has been the case in many other cultures. Other groups of words refer more specifically to contemporary conditions. *Bureaucracy, bureaucrat, bureaucratism*, all derived from the French *bureau*, suggest that the modern image of authority is a man seated behind a desk rather than one mounted on a horse. Connected with *bureau* in the same semantic area are terms like *file, register, classification*, all implying the aim to put things and people into neat categories. On the other hand there are many groups of words in contemporary usage which suggest that authority is based on common consent and working together for the common good. Such words could also be grouped together for semantic analysis. Many of them in the European languages have prefixes meaning with or together, e.g., English *co*operation, *com*mission, *col*lective, *com*munal, *co*-existence, *com*munism. It would be interesting, indeed, to make a comparative study for the equivalents of such terms in two or more languages outside the Indo-European family.

3. GENERAL REASONS FOR CHANGE OF MEANING

A word as a linguistic sign, though generally intelligible in a given speech community, is never uttered twice under exactly the same circumstances. This is simply because no human situation can possibly repeat itself with all environmental factors the same. Such an elementary fact of our existence would seem to imply that communication among people by language must by its very nature be very inaccurate and frustrating. But the situation is really not so desperate. The social give-and-take of speakers in a community which share general experiences will tend to establish a norm and to eliminate accidental or freakish usages from common acceptance: as if, for instance, a woman in a shop said "I want to try on that cat" while pointing to a hat. Her slip of the tongue would be readily corrected.

Nevertheless there are varying degrees of stability in the use of words. Stability means lack of ambiguity. The terminology of the natural sciences may be said to offer the most stable words of all. When a research worker in a laboratory says "The temperature is now 20° centigrade," a listener obtains a very precise message from him. The words *temperature* and *centigrade* are clearly defined and understood. It is convenient to say that they have a clear denotation.

Later in the day, however, the same research worker may say to a friend "The weather is depressing" or "Your suggestion is fantastic" or "That novel is really decadent." Here the key terms *depressing* and *fantastic* and *decadent* are not so easily pinned down as are centigrades. All three of them have an aura of associations which may be called their connotations: that is, meanings implied if not strictly defined in relation to the terms.

Connotation or multiple associations of a word will in general facilitate a shift in its meaning. The phenomenon can be observed particularly in words which are associated with the emotions. Old English had a compounded noun *lēofmann* which meant simply a dear person, whether man or woman. Originally a very dignified term, applicable even in a religious context, it later became limited to erotic relationships referring only to a sweetheart or lover. By Chaucer's time the epithet (then pronounced *lemman*) had assumed such vulgar connotations that the poet apologized for using it, maintaining however that it alone was appropriate in the interests of honest realism for the scene he was describing. On the other hand words like *boat, hammer, house* refer to the same classes of objects that they designated over a thousand years ago, with no change of meaning.

When the relation between sign and referent is clear and unambiguous, we customarily say that the one denotes the other. When however the sign evokes in addition various associations (psychological and social, shall we say), then it is said to connote them. But denotation and connotation cannot be sharply distinguished. Actually the vocabulary of any language represents a spectrum of terms ranging from the most precisely denotative to the most richly and confusingly connotative: for example from *erg* at one end to *God* or *spirit* on the other. The historical results of connotation throughout human history seem to have been portentous, though hard to estimate. At least it may be said that wars have never been fought over such issues as the definition of an *erg*, but they have been waged—at least so far as the participants were consciously aware—over varying definitions of *God*. The social implications of connotation would seem to be serious indeed.

Yet one should be careful about trying to evaluate the historical results of linguistic connotation. During the 1930's, especially in America, there was a group of writers interested in semantics, who formulated the doctrine that connotational obscurities are the root of social evils, and that if all basic terms (especially slogans current in political and economic controversy) were clearly defined and understood, then all basic problems of human relationships would be automatically solved. Presumably, a cool joint discussion of the terms Allah and God by Saracens and Christians might have prevented the Crusades, and an obligation on the part of Hitler to define clearly and scientifically such terms as Aryan or racial purity or international Jewish capitalism would have frustrated the entire Nazi program, thus avoiding the worst catastrophe which mankind has ever endured.

Now it is no doubt true that denotative definitions are desirable, and they serve to clarify issues and actions in all fields of human endeavour. But at the same time there are other factors outside of semantics which fundamentally shape the history of mankind. We dare not overlook them. No doubt many Christians enlisted in the Crusades out of a sincere desire to further their conception of the term God as opposed to the Saracens' term Allah. Nevertheless we know that there were also deep-lying economic causes, having to do with hindrances to East-West trade, which help to explain why the slogan about rescuing the Holy Sepulchre became emotionally explosive just when it did. And to understand the success of Hitler's deplorable jargon one has to recall the economic situation in Germany of the 1920's. The consequences of the Versailles Treaty (against which the well-informed English bourgeois economist John Meynard Keynes early voiced warnings), the impact of world-wide depression and unemployment on a country already handicapped by defeat and post-war restrictions—all these extralinguistic factors must be taken into account if one is to understand the acceptance of Hitler's glaringly unscientific terminology by a major part of a people that also prided itself on scientific understanding and linguistic discipline.

The main proponent of so-called "general semantics" in America, namely Alfred Korzybski, has attracted a number of followers; together they form a school which claims to represent a new (non-Aristotelian) philosophical approach to language and society. Actually their analyses are often superficial and their deductions are misleading: the former cloaked in pretentious language are banal when they are sound; and the latter are dangerous because they distort (by oversimplification) the picture of social forces at work in today's world. From the strictly scientific point of view, Korzybski's school is hardly worth mentioning; but it has had and apparently continues to have a considerable influence in the West.[2]

The reasons for changes of meaning of words are multiple and various. To describe all of them adequately would require wide excursions into the area of social history, in order to correlate it with linguistics. However, two general causes may be distinguished. In the one case, an old linguistic sign continues to be used with reference to a new object or process or relationship in the external world of experience, long after the old reference has become anachronistic. In the second case, a linguistic sign is itself subject to change, and thus its reference may become obscured or trans-

---

[2] For a summary of Korzybski's self-styled "non-Aristotelian" theory of general semantics see Adam Schaff, *Wstęp do Semantyki* (Warsaw, 1960), pp. 38–64; English translation, *Introduction to Semantics*. The present writer published a negative estimate some years ago: "Semantics as Social Evasion," *Science and Society*, VI (1942), 315 ff.

ferred. In other words, the first general cause is extra-linguistic, while the second is primarily linguistic.

Examples of old terms applied to new objects (or activities or relationships or intellectual concepts) are very easily found. Long ago steamboats replaced sailboats; but in English one still speaks of setting sail on a boat that has no sail at all. For centuries people wrote with sharpened feathers, as witness the words *pen* (from Latin *penna*), *plume, Feder, pióro*. We still use those words although the feathers have long since been rejected in favour of plastic fountain-pens, ballpoint pens and typewriters. In early times the thorn (Latin *spīna*) may have served to hold together bits of clothing, or at least it served as a model for primitive devices made out of bone for the same purpose. Today we have French *épingle*, derived from *spīnula* "little thorn," but referring to delicate steel instruments of quite a different character. In various languages there are terms equivalent to sunrise and sunset, although we have known since the time of Copernicus that it is the earth that moves, not the sun in relation to it. Finally it may be pointed out that the word *atom* comes from Greek ἄτομος or *a-tom-os*, meaning that which cannot be divided—yet we use the term now, long after the famous splitting of the so-called atom made the word an anachronism.

Changed linguistic signs may cause shifts and confusions too. As the sounds of a language gradually change, previous distinctions may be lost for purely phonological reasons. Thus arise homonyms or similar-sounding pairs of words which affect each other's meaning even though the two in question were originally quite unrelated. In Old English the word *stigel* (connected with German *steigen*) meant a set of steps for climbing over a fence. In the course of time it came to be pronounced identically with the word *style*, from a Greek-derived Latin term meaning a pointed tool for writing (*stylus*). Therefore the poet Chaucer was able to make a humorous punning reference to literary "high-style" as if it had something to do with climbing over a fence from one field to another. The English word *grave*, from Latin *gravis* (meaning heavy) is associated by phonological similarity with another word *grave* (meaning tomb; *graef* from the Old English verb *grafan*, to dig; compare Polish *grób*). The two are not connected but they are sure to exert a mutual semantic influence because of similarity of sound. Association by such phonetic similarity has affected the reference of *brothel*, a native English word which once meant any kind of base, lewd person. By confusion with French *bordel* it came to be applied to the house frequented by lewd persons for a specific purpose: that is, a house of prostitution. Again, the English words *ridge* and *rigid* come from quite different sources. The former, allied with German *Rücken*, and once pronounced *hrycg*, was primarily applied to the back of a person or an animal, then extended to the "back" of a range of mountains: that is the series of its summits. The latter, ultimately from Latin *rigidus*, means stiff, unyielding. Sound changes operating independently in the two languages (English and Latin) have brought the two forms together. The non-morpheme *rig-* of the Latin loan words is now associated with the homonymous full morpheme *ridge*, so that on hearing the expression "He is very rigid in his opinions" a listener may readily understand the expression in the sense of stiff-backed, and even visualize a mountainous horizon as a symbolic equivalent of the adjective, apprehended pictorially.

4. MAIN TYPES OF SEMANTIC CHANGE

There are many specific types of semantic change brought about by shifting relations between sign and referent. Attempts to classify them under clear and mutually exclusive headings are hopeless, because more than one factor often comes into play in a given instance, and the results of the change may frequently be variously described. The following list of types follows traditional categories, but some attempt will be made to indicate overlappings.

Meliorative semantic change occurs when a word or expression is elevated from a humbler meaning to one more exalted. A classical example current in many languages today is the elevation of the Greek *angelos*, originally meaning a simple messenger (nothing more exalted than a modern postman) to a term designating an intermediary between divine mind and human mind. The elevation is due to a combination of Neo-Platonic philosophy and early Christian ideology in the late Roman empire. It involves also a transition from concrete to abstract meaning (about which more later).—The humble Old English word *stiweard* was once a compound expression with the literal sense of a supervisor (warden or guard) of an enclosure for cattle or pigs (compare *-sty* in modern *pigsty*). But later a steward came to mean an administrator of a large estate; and in a modified form, Stuart, it was the patronymic of a powerful dynasty of English monarchs in the 17th century, representatives in fact of the doctrine of the divine right of kings. From pigsty to royal palace: truly a dazzling meliorative change.

Pejorative change is the opposite of meliorative. It occurs when words or expressions are degraded from a higher semantic field to a lower one—speaking in terms of social connotation, of course. Here it is even easier to find examples than in the area of meliorative change. The word *lemman*, already cited (sec. 3) is a case in point. It is interesting to note in the light of social history, that words associated with rural occupations have been especially subject to pejorative change in the era since the towns and cities began to represent livelier centres of cultural life than the village: that is, during the later Middle Ages. Thus English *boor*, cognate with German *Bauer*, meant originally simply a tiller of the soil (surely a laudable occupation), but today an uncultivated person. Similarly English *pagan*, from the Latin *pāgānus*, meant simply a countryman. But since Christianity reached the villages somewhat later than the towns, the term was likewise subject to pejorative semantic change. One might compare the deterioration of the English word *heathen*, literally meaning a resident on the heath or in the wilderness. So likewise the word *churl*, cognate with German *Kerl* and the name *Karl*, has deteriorated along with *boor*. An interesting social attitude is revealed in the history of the Polish word for a madman, *wariat*. It comes from the Latin *variāre*, meaning simply to vary, to be different (from other people, in this case). Similarly *idiot* comes from Greek *idiōtēs* a private person; hence one who is ignorant because he keeps himself aloof (from public affairs, among other things). The two pejorative changes represent group disapproval of non-conformity in behaviour.

Extension of meaning may often be observed. The Latin word *causa* was applied primarily to cases at law; one would say that a *causa* was before a judge. But Italian *cosa* and French *chose*, contemporary descendants of the term, simply mean a thing. The English word *thing* itself, like German *Ding*, was once limited to a meeting or a discussion. German *Sache* (compare English *sake*) originally had the same meaning as *causa*; the semantic widening is the same in all these instances. Polish *rzecz*, originally signifying a word or speech, has had an analogous history of generalization.

Restriction of meaning, on the other hand, may be illustrated by English *meat*, which is today usually limited to flesh food but originally meant food in general, as is indicated in the archaic phrase *meat and drink*. Polish has borrowed Latin *collātiō*, which meant a gathering together of people or things, and narrowed it down to the gathering of food at a specific time, namely for the evening meal. Latin *fractiō* could mean the breaking of anything, but in English *fraction* means only a broken number in the terminology of arithmetic. Polish *czas* has preserved the general sense of time, while Russian has restricted the same word to a limited subdivision of time, namely an hour.

Ellipsis or omission of words normally juxtaposed may affect the meaning of the words retained. One result may be, in effect, extension of meaning. A striking example is offered by the present-day usage of the word *nuclear*. The noun *nucleus* from which this adjective is derived, meant in Latin a little nut; hence the kernel of any plant; hence finally the central part of an ultimate unit of matter, namely the atom. Since the application of nuclear physics to modern techniques of war, the adjective in question is used as an elliptical term to relate specifically to those techniques. Thus a nuclear power means one possessed of atomic bombs (not, as one might expect, a tiny, unimportant power), and so on. In French, the ellipsis of a negative word has converted its traditional partner into an opposite meaning, at least in certain contexts.

French *personne*, according to its origin in Roman usage, meant a mask or a character in a play, and later a human individual. This was a case of semantic extension. The expression *ne... personne* (as in: *il n'y a personne*; *je ne vois personne*) meant nobody. But the negative may be suppressed in certain situations, for instance in answers to questions. In answer to the query *Qui est là?* the reply may be, *Personne*. Literally, if one thinks of the word's history, this might be expected to mean somebody, but in contemporary French usage it means the opposite: nobody. In current English, the phrase *pulmonary tuberculosis* or *tuberculosis of the lungs* has been abbreviated to simple *tuberculosis* or *consumption* (for *consumption of the lungs*) with resultant restriction of meaning. In America the term *Indian corn* was originally applied to maize, a special variety of cereal grain. Later the adjective was omitted. Thus *corn*, originally signifying any kind of grain (wheat, oats, etc.) came to be restricted to one.

Metaphor or transfer of meaning plays a considerable part in the semantic history of words. The most obvious (and perhaps the most primitive?) examples concern the transfer of terms for parts of the human body to external objects in nature. Thus in English one speaks of the lip of a crater, the eye of a potato, the mouth of a tunnel or a river, the foot of a mountain and so on. Here we have to do with extension of meaning by a very special method of analogy.

Abstraction of meaning may also occur. A concrete word or expression, once very limited in its reference, may be extended to wide spheres of intellectual activity. Religious terminology offers many examples. The shift may at the same time be amelioration, as in the case of *angel*, already cited, or *redemption*, with its basic literal sense of buying something back. Terms for intellectual activity have sometimes been abstracted from physical ones: Latin *dis-cernere* (from which English *discern*) and its Greek cognate *krinein* have a basic sense to separate (physical objects, such as wheat from chaff); thence, the ability to distinguish, to observe differences under seeming likenesses, to analyze. Curiously, the same development of ideas can be noticed in the Icelandic word *skilja* which means to separate, to distinguish, and also to understand. Here too there is a certain type of metaphorical comparison of the physical with the intellectual.

5. SOME SPECIAL FACTORS OF SOCIAL ENVIRONMENT

The examples quoted above will have indicated how many complex psychological factors operate when words change meaning. One thing is clear, however. All changes of whatever sort must be accepted by a social community if they are to be effective. Individual aberrations and innovations mean nothing unless they are taken over by a wider group. And when they are, some very special factors may operate which are related to the way of living and the way of looking at things on the part of given communities.

This brings us back to a consideration of the collective attitudes of people living together which may produce or at least accelerate some of the general types of semantic change noted in the preceding section.

Fear is one motive which may affect the use of words. Among primitive men, it seems, there was a general conviction that a name had a powerful magic connexion with the person or thing signified. If you knew the name of your enemy you could curse him and perhaps destroy him; if not, you had less power over him. If you mentioned the name of a god or demon directly, you might stimulate him to alarming activity: hence it was better to avoid direct reference and substitute a paraphrase. Fear and extreme reverence could be combined. The classical example is the Hebrew cluster of four written consonants, variously transliterated (in English as Jehovah) which stood for the name of God, too sacred to be pronounced; hence synonyms were produced to replace it (e.g. Adonai, meaning Lord). Fear of death, as of a kind of personalized force, is still operative among many people who consider themselves far above the primitive level. English is full of substitute phrases. During the first World War, soldiers did not die, but "went West"; in American slang they "kicked the bucket." Even now people are said "to pass away," or "leave us," or the like, instead of "to die" in the phraseology of some over-elegant (or over-fearful?) speakers.

Tabu is a term (derived from the Polynesian languages) applied to something sacred and also forbidden. Words themselves may become tabu because of their connotations, and thus pass out of usage. Their substitutes may in turn be subjected to the same elimination. Thus a recurrent shift of vocabulary may occur because of fear of that which is tabu.

Prudery is still another motive which may cause shifts and substitutions in vocabulary. Physiological functions not considered fitting for public execution—mostly those related to sex, defecation and urination—have a terminology particularly subject to pejorative change. A dual vocabulary may arise, as in English: a purely scientific colourless one that may be used without offense in polite conversation, and a set of popular synonyms which are considered unacceptable in the same sort of conversation. But the popular synonyms may be so widely extended in a metaphorical sense as to become greatly weakened semantically. In general, when an unpleasant topic is alluded to indirectly by periphrases and substitute expressions the linguistic result is called an euphemism. The social motives may be various (fear, courtesy, prudery, etc.).

Social specialization of vocabulary may occur besides the kind just mentioned. In some types of society there is a special set of words which are used only by women, who keep them secret from the men. Men for their part have been known to keep terminology such as that of initiation rites and of warfare (names of weapons and the like) as a secret from outsiders. The vocabulary of children, although not secret, is often very special. And finally there are the jargons attached to various trades and professions, incomprehensible to an outsider. These often embrace generally current words or expressions applied in a special way. Thus in English the phrase "on the rocks" normally means what it says, literally; but in the jargon of professional bartenders it has come to mean "on ice"—a specialized metaphorical usage. Conversely, expressions once limited to the jargon of a special occupation may be widened. In American English the expression "step on the gas" originated as part of the technical phraseology connected with the driving of automobiles; today it is widely current in colloquial

speech as an equivalent of the verb *hurry* (especially as an imperative). Here also a metaphor is involved, of course. The adoption of
it was conditioned by the tremendous growth of automotive transportation in this century. Should another means of locomotion
replace it, the expression would no doubt become obsolete.

Social ambition, or the desire to appear more elegant, important
or powerful than one really is, may find expression in semantic
usage. The result may be a weakening of the meaning due to over-ex-
pansion, as when the title *esquire*, once reserved for a candidate
for knighthood or a landed proprietor, has been so extended in
England—at least in addressing the envelope of a letter—that it has
become almost synonymous with the universally applicable Mr.
(When so used, Esquire is abbreviated Esq. and written after the
person's name, not before.) The basic social motive may have been
courtesy rather than self-aggrandizement. One may compare the
tendency in Polish usage to address any official with the title
appropriate to the rank above him: a *naczelnik* as *dyrektor*,
a *docent* as *profesor*, and so on. The motive of self-aggrandizement
is, however, quite clearly evident in some neologisms recently
noted in America. Garbage men (that is, collectors of refuse) in
a certain city have asked officially to be called "public works com-
bustible fieldmen." Janitors (concierges) of even modest buildings
now want to be called custodians, a title formerly associated with
keepers of large public buildings or collections of cultural importance: for instance rare manuscripts or objects of art. An interesting
example is offered by the history and present use of the word
undertaker. By origin it meant nothing more than a person who
assumes a task (any task) to be performed. Later it was restricted
to mean someone who prepares the dead for burial and funeral
ceremonies. But the native English word has been replaced in
America by a neologism, *mortician*. Since it rimes with such impressive words as *statistician*, *theoretician* and *phonetician*, it
suggests a lofty kind of specialization. Here another factor must be
taken into account. Fear of mentioning death, even indirectly,
would hasten the substitution of a new term for the current and
familiar one. But curiously enough the older word *undertaker* has

no etymological connexion with death, whereas the neologism *mortician* contains a Latin element, identifiable in English *mort-al*, which means precisely: death.

Just as the types of semantic change overlap, so do their social motivations. It is clear from all that has been said that the area of semantics offers many problems for future investigation. It may be said, in fact, that we have just made a beginning in the study of this fascinating field of linguistic research.

CHAPTER 5

THE SOUNDS OF A LANGUAGE: RECORDING AND
TRANSCRIPTION

1. EARLY FORMS OF ALPHABETS

For unnumbered millenia, it seems, human beings have been making use of the highly conventionalized method of communication known as oral speech. But they were slow in elaborating methods of recording their speech in written forms.

Picture writing seems to have been the earliest method of making records. It would be possible, for instance, to record pictorially the fact that "The King received tribute of corn and cows from his vassals" by showing a monarch seated on his throne, and a series of humble individuals offering the goods concerned. The amount or number of goods could be indicated by a very primitive representation of counting. Let us remember that the Roman numeral for five, namely V, is based on a picture symbol for an open hand with five fingers extended, while that for ten, X, is a combination of two such open hands. Various number systems based on fives, tens and twenties go back to the elementary fact that early man began to count with the aid of his fingers and toes.

In picture writing, things and actions are most readily depicted and most easily interpreted. A figure such as ◉ or ◎ is readily understood to stand for the human eye; the addition of signs for drops of water below the eye can as readily convert this into a figure meaning to weep: ◉ . Of course such images give no clue to the words which were used in converting the signs into oral messages. For that very reason picture writing, even when greatly stylized, can serve as an intertribal means of communication among speakers of quite different languages. If for instance a figure like ⚲ standing for "man with scepter, king" were prefixed or suffixed to the sign for "to weep," then any recipient of the message would translate it aloud into a sentence equivalent of "the king weeps," regardless of the specific noun or verb used in his own spoken language.

A pictorial sign used to represent a class of objects or a type of action rather than single concrete objects or events is called an ideogram. Thus the figure 👁 represents weeping in general, not necessarily the weeping of a specific tribesman X. Herein lies the possibility for further generalization.

We may clearly trace the process of generalization, leading to the formation of an alphabet, in the ancient Egyptian language. By an alphabet we usually understand a series of signs which correspond to individual sounds in a language, or to syllables, rather than to things or actions being referred to. The transition from picture signs to letters of an alphabet represented an enormous step forward in the history of human communication. How did it occur?

Variously in various cultures, obviously; but perhaps the best example is, as has been said, the development of ancient Egyptian writing. Here as in Semitic languages, consonants alone were regarded as essential in transcribing a word. Now it happens that Egyptian had many monosyllabic words that were homonyms at least as far as their consonantal structure was concerned. The ideogram picturing the bird swallow stood for the word *w-r*; but *w-r* also meant big; therefore the bird ideogram could be used for the adjective. In English the noun *swallow* has a homonym in the verb *to swallow*. If today's languages were to be obliged to evolve from picture writing to alphabet, we can imagine the following combinations of signs recurring:

🦅 : the bird swallow

🦅 ι : swallow+tail (a swallow-tail suit worn by modern gentlemen on formal occasions)

🦅➡ : to swallow a fish.

In the last expression, the verb meaning to swallow food has obviously nothing to do with the bird, but homonyms permit the ready substitution of ideograms. Or we can imagine the following analogous development if contemporary Polish were to begin to evolve now from ideograms to writing. Let us imagine that a character like ▦ were used to designate *wy* in the sense of "you, all of you together," and that a character like 𝄇 (a mouth with words coming out of it) were used to designate *rzec*, the act of talking. The two together might thus be interpreted as "you speak." But the pronoun *wy* has a homonymous Polish morpheme *wy*—meaning out of, proceeding from, etc. Hence the word *wyrzec* (meaning to resign from something) would also be rendered by the two symbols suggested, thus: 𝄇𝄇 even though the prefix to the verb has nothing to do semantically with the homonymous pronoun *wy*.

At this stage one may say that we have reached syllabic writing. A language comparatively rich in homonymous morphemes will naturally lend itself better to syllabic transcription than others. English has very many homonymous word-morphemes which could be reduced to single ideograms. In the following list, the word having concrete connotations is given first, since it would be better adapted to ideographic transcription:

> *bee* (the noun): *be* (the verb denoting existence, being, etc.)
> *buy* (the verb): *by* (the preposition)
> *fare* (the verb): *fair* (the adjective)
> *loan* (the verb or noun): *lone* (the adjective)
> *pail* (the noun): *pale* (the adjective)
> *way* (the noun): *weigh* (the verb).

The next stage in Egyptian was to make letters out of one-consonant sound-symbols, thus yielding an alphabet of 24 letters (as if the picture of a bee, for instance, were taken to stand for the sound *b* wherever it occurred). Along with retained signs indicating more than one sound, like ⊏⊐ standing for *p-r* (originally "house") with any combination of adjacent vowels, it made wide use of signs indicating simple consonants: ⊓ (a stool) for *p*, ⊸ (a mouth) for *r*, and so on.

Because there may be many homonyms in a written language like Egyptian—the more so if only consonants are recorded—it is sometimes desirable to indicate by a sign of some sort the semantic area to which a given word belongs. The conventional image of the sun ⊙ associated with the consonantal roots *hrw* "day" and *wbn* "rise, shine" served to avoid confusion with other like roots of different meanings. Such images, of no phonetic value, are called classifiers or determinants. Chinese script, which is today very conventional though descended from a form of picture writing, uses some such indicators to distinguish among multiple groups of homonyms. Since the spoken word *shan* may mean either a shirt or a mountain, with no difference in musical pitch between the two, a symbol (*kien*), meaning an article of clothing, is prefixed to the word in the former sense, and another (*tso*), meaning site or location, to its homonym in the latter sense. Other visual devices are also employed to reduce the confusion.

Picture writing has sometimes developed towards alphabetic writing by a different method, namely the substitution of like-sounding syllables instead of homonymous full words. This is known as the rebus method. Among the ancient Aztecs of Mexico a pictograph representing a banner stood for the word *pa-ntli*, but was later used for the syllable *pa-* in general; the pictograph of a stone, *te-tl* could similarly stand for the syllable *te-* in other contexts. Therefore the combination of a banner-sign and a stone-sign could represent a word *pa-te* (in this case, a borrowing from Latin *pater*) which had nothing to do with either image. Rebus writing, being related to the sounds of human speech, had obvious advantages over picture writing, but it still suffered from obvious shortcomings. To be effective it had to produce a sign for every possible syllable in a given language: and that might require very many signs indeed.

An alphabet, on the other hand, is designed to represent not images or groups of homonymous words or like-sounding syllables, but the individual sounds of a language. Once these are identified, even approximatively, it will be found that the number is very few, even where the inventory is relatively great, in comparison with the number of words or homonyms or different syllables in the same language. It was the speakers of ancient Phoenician, or of another Semitic language closely allied to it, who seem to have made the decisive transition towards an alphabet as we understand the term. The Phoenician characters are akin to those found on early inscriptions in Crete and on Mount Sinai; these in turn show relationships with some Egyptian hieroglyphs. From the Phoenicians (probably) the Greeks took over and modified the originally Semitic alphabet for their own uses. Not all of the connexions are clear, but even today some of them are obvious. Our very word alphabet comes from two Semitic words (compare Hebrew *āleph* and *bēth*) for the first two letters. The first of them almost certainly meant an ox, and early forms of the character ∀ ∀ ⅄ ⋗ ⊿ A show a likeness to the animals' head, as indeed does our modern A (although now turned upside down). The Greek Δ (*delta*; Hebrew *dāleth*), has the same shape in Phoenician and Cretan inscriptions, though it appears on its side as ◁ in some of the former. Greek M (*mu*; Hebrew *mēm*) is related to Sinaitic ∿ and Phoenician ⸗, signs for water. What is important is that the Greeks established a clear relation between individual sounds and signs, not only for consonants but vowels. In only a few cases, such as Ψ (*psi*), a single sign represented more than one sound.

The Greek alphabet was transplanted to Italy and was there adapted to an early form of Latin. Here a number of changes in use and interpretation occurred, but many of the signs were but slightly modified, if at all. From the Greek characters, with additions, is derived the medieval Cyrillic still used today in slightly modified form for such Slavic languages as Russian, Ukrainian and Bulgarian. From the Latin (sometimes with modifications as in the case of Polish) is derived the basic alphabet common to languages of Western and Central Europe, the New World, and parts of Asia and Africa.

For many early systems of writing, the technological medium used was decisive for determining the nature of the characters. Carving with a chisel on stone or painting with a brush or scratching on the surface of wood are three different techniques illustrated by ancient Egyptian, Chinese, and primitive Germanic writings. The last-named were recorded in the so-called runic alphabet, which avoided curved lines and specialized in angular formations. The cuneiform writings of Assyria and Babylonia used clusters of wedge-shaped strokes originally inscribed by a stylus on clay tablets; these were later (as in Persia) adapted to stone. The technique of writing on medieval manuscripts reflects the use of pen and ink. Modern printing has further modified the traditional Latin alphabet, making its characters clearer and more readily distinguished than they were in late medieval script.

2. ALPHABETS AND SOUNDS TODAY

Although the Greek and Latin alphabets represented a great achievement in the history of human culture, neither was completely unambiguous. Moreover, the traditional orthography, once established, continued to be used after the spoken sounds changed very perceptibly, as they were sure to do in the course of centuries, not to say millenia. In time the discrepancy between speaking and writing in any set of characters may become very great unless the orthography is deliberately revised. The second letter of the early Semitic alphabet as adapted by the Greeks was known as *bēta*. This was a sign-word originally standing for a house (compare Hebrew *bēth*) and as the letter *B* it stood for the initial sound of that word. It retained that value in Latin and the languages descended from Latin. But in spoken Greek the sound *b* had regularly developed into *v* by the early Middle Ages. In adapting the Greek letters for the establishment of a Slavic alphabet, St. Cyril quite properly equated *B* with the contemporary Slavic sound *v*; and since Slavic also had a *b*-sound (by this time lacking in Greek) he created a new letter *Б* (obviously a modified form of the old *bēta*) to represent it. He was also careful to create other letters for other sounds not represented in ninth-century Greek.

This was an instance of unusual revision and adaptation. Very often however the use of alphabetic characters ignores very fundamental changes in pronunciation. Modern English and French, with their conservative orthography, are glaring examples of such archaism in spelling. (See ch. 1, sec. 1.) The English still write the word *knight* as they did in the late Middle Ages (at which time consonants were actually sounded to correspond with the *k* and the *gh*), although they now say something more like *nait*. The French write *nouveaux* with eight letters when they say something like *nuvo* (with accent on the second syllable). Other modern languages employing forms of the Latin alphabet use them in much closer correlation with spoken sounds: among others, Italian, Spanish, Polish, German, Hungarian. But among these too there are many discrepancies in the orthographic treatment of certain sounds. The combination of letters *ch* represents three different values in Spanish, Italian and German respectively; *s* and *sz* have differing, interchanged values in Polish and Hungarian. Confusion was rendered much worse when attempts were made to employ the limited Latin alphabet to record quite exotic languages such as those of the Indians in North and South America, of native peoples in Africa and Asia. Traditional Latin writing simply did not offer enough distinctive signs for the purpose.

An amplified system was obviously needed in order to transcribe not only the languages of Europe but those of other continents as well. A system designed to fit such broad demands had to meet two requirements: (1) it had to be self-consistent and unambiguous, so that students of all countries might be able to interpret it in the same way; (2) it had to be efficient—which meant in practice the use of a single symbol to represent a single sound. According to the second principle such spellings as *th* in English or *sz* in Polish would be eliminated, since in each case two letters were being used for one sound.

In response to the new—if rather belated—awareness of the need indicated, an important society called the International Phonetic Association was founded in 1886. It drew up an international alphabet of characters (1888) by which, it was stated, "the pronunciation of any language may be accurately represented." In view of the then prevailing confusions, this was an aim both desirable and long overdue. The relatively recent date serves to remind us once more how young is the science known as linguistics. The Association published a journal, called *Le Maître phonétique*, which included articles and also transcribed texts from a wide range of previously little-known languages (e.g., Aleutian, Burmese, Chinese in several forms, Japanese, Javanese, etc.), all in the standard international alphabet. Such texts were given in what was known as "broad transcription." For purposes of "narrow transcription," designed to record more detailed nuances of pronunciation, the Association proposed a series of additional symbols which were mostly slight variations of the major ones. The International Phonetic Alphabet (IPA) was soon used to excellent effect in dictionaries of pronunciation for a number of languages.

One main purpose of the IPA was, as was said, to avoid waste and ambiguity by following the principle of using one character— and one only—for one sound. It would avoid such spellings as English *th*, a combination of two letters conventionally used for two distinctly different single sounds, as in *thistle* as compared with *this*. In the IPA the Greek letter θ was borrowed to represent the initial consonant of the first word, and the Old English character ð to represent that of the second.

Besides adhering to the principle of one character for one sound, the Association also presented characters standing for all sounds in a logical order related to their modes of articulation, not in the haphazard order to which users of the modified Greek and Latin alphabet are accustomed. (As has been mentioned in ch. 1, only one ancient alphabet, the Sanskrit, had anticipated the demand for such systematic ordering. That alphabet was an extraordinary scientific achievement.) Thus, for consonants, it appeared far more sensible to arrange them in an order related to the speech organs primarily employed in producing them, for instance:

Lips   p   b   f   v   m
Teeth   t   d   θ   ð   n

and so on down to those pronounced deepest in the throat. At the same time one could distinguish, in columns, between consonants made without vibration of the vocal cords (called voiceless) from those made with such vibration (called voiced); likewise between those articulated by a brief impact of air on the speech organs (called stops or plosives) and those which are prolonged (called spirants or fricatives). Thus:

	Stops		Spirants	
	Voiceless	Voiced	Voiceless	Voiced
Lips	p	b	f	v
Teeth	t	d	θ	ð

The (usually) voiced consonants produced by sending the air through the nose with the tongue at various positions, called nasals, could be set apart as a special category of spirants including m, n, p (the last corresponding to the sound represented by Spanish ñ, French *gn*) and ŋ (corresponding to English *ng* in *sing*). Vowels too could be arranged according to the positions of the tongue, the position of the jaws, the degree of sounding of the lips, as for instance:

Front, high, unrounded: i   Front, high, rounded: u

Front, mid, unrounded: e   Front, mid, rounded: o

The vowels and consonants here cited are but illustrative examples, chosen because the characters used for them are already familiar in conventional alphabets. Actually, the languages of the world include a very wide range of sounds, distinguishable in some cases by extremely subtle nuances of articulation. Very many new characters had to be devised for the IPA in order to provide for new speech sounds being recorded as the study of previously unknown languages communities progressed throughout the world.

A truly international phonetic alphabet must indeed have something of a universal, even an absolute character. That is to say, it undertakes to record specific variations of pronunciation regardless whether they are important in a given language or not. In Polish for instance, it is important to distinguish between two kinds of *l*, one made with the front part of the tongue (printed as *l*) and another made with the back part of the tongue (printed as *l*). The difference between these two articulations is essential in the Polish language. Otherwise, if they are confused, a listener will not know whether his interlocutor is saying "I sat on the lava" (Polish *lawa*) or "I sat on the bench" (Polish *lawa*). But in English the verb "to love" will be understood unambiguously whether one says "I love you" or "I love you." The latter pronunciation might be considered quaint or foreign, but would not lead to any misunderstanding as to the speaker's message. In other words, the distinction is non-essential for English though clearly essential for Polish. In the IPA, as used in transcription of modern German, two different signs are used for the final consonants of *ich* and *auch.* The former, appearing only after vowels articulated at the front of the mouth, is transcribed as [ç], while the latter, appearing only after vowels articulated at the back of the mouth, is transcribed as [χ]. However, if a speaker of German said the word *ich* with the back consonant [χ], he would be understood without difficulty, though he might—as in the case of a speaker of English confusing *l* and *ł*—be charged with an odd or foreign enunciation. There would be no danger of confusion with another word. Within a given language it is one thing to show minor unessential deviations from the accepted pattern and quite another thing to introduce deviations which lead to confusion, especially confusion of one word with another.

But what is essential in one language may be quite unessential in another. In describing a specific language it is desirable to concentrate first of all upon the units of speech-sound which serve to distinguish words and other morphemes from one another. These minimal units of relevant contrast in sound are called phonemes as opposed to phonetic units. Two of the latter which differ only according to the environment in which they are found, like the various articulations of English *l* in proximity to front or back vowels (e.g. *will* versus *cool*; or German *ich* versus *auch*) are called conditioned variants or allophones of the same phoneme. If two variations occur in mutually exclusive environments—again, let us say, in proximity to front versus back vowels—they are also said to be in complementary distribution. Complementary distribution simply means that in an environment where you find one sound (Polish [l], German [ç] near front vowels like [i]), you won't find another phonetically related sound (never Polish [ł] or German [χ], which belong near back vowels like [u]). A phonemic transcription, then, will use a single character to subsume all conditioned variants, disregarding irrelevant nuances. It is customary to place the signs for phonemes within slanting lines, e.g. [l], thus representing all varieties of the English phoneme. A phonetic transcription which distinguishes among conditioned variants of a single phoneme is placed within square brackets, as with German [ç] and [χ] cited above.

It may happen that two separate sounds that are phonetically distinct but clearly associated in articulation can function as single phonemes. The two English words *shin* and *chin* are distinguished by the fact that the first begins with a hissing voiceless spirant sound transcribed as [ʃ] while the second begins with a combination represented as [tʃ]—the same spirant preceded by a similarly articulated stop. Since the contrast serves to distinguish many word pairs in English (*share* : *chair*; *shatter* : *chatter*; *shanty*: *chanty*) there is good reason to regard [tʃ] as a single phoneme and to use a single character, namely /č/ in transcribing it. In the Bantu languages /mb/ and /nd/ function as single phonemes. In German the combination of labial voiceless stop and corresponding voiceless spirant [pf] is very frequent. That it has a claim to phonemic status may be demonstrated by contrasting the words *Pfand* and *fand*. In English also two sounds [p] and [f] may be found in sequence as in the word *cupful*, but here we deny the combination phonemic status because it does not appear within the same morpheme and does not contrast consistently with other single phonemes in the formation of morphemes.

A phonemic description ignoring conditioned variants, will be found concise and efficient for the recording of a language at a specific period of time. On the other hand, when it is desired to account for the history of sounds in the same language over a period of several centuries, the description may have to be more strictly phonetic. At an earlier period in the history of English, the single sound now usually represented by the spelling *ng*, namely [ŋ] as in *sing*, appeared only before the consonants *k* and *g*. The word *sing* was then pronounced [siŋg]. Thus the [ŋ] was merely a conditioned variant of [n] and both consonants could have been at that time subsumed as a single phoneme /n/. But later on the final *g*'s of words like *sing* were lost. As a result, the original variant [ŋ] became a phoneme /ŋ/ in its own right, since it now served to distinguish such word-pairs as *sin* and *sing*, *run* and *rung*.

Pairs of words which are identical except for one sound, like *sin* and *sing* just cited, are used in drawing up the inventory of phonemes in a given language. They are called minimal pairs. However it will be found that some phonemes contrast with many others, while a certain number contrast with very few. The frequency with which a phoneme appears in minimal pairs is sometimes called its functional yield. English /b/ contrasts initially with many other consonants as well as with zero (that is, no consonant at all) as can be seen by comparing *bin* with the words *in, din, fin, gin* (pronounced [dʒin], phonemically transcribed /ǯin/, *kin, linn, pin, sin, tin, win*. On the other hand the /ž/-sound alone, corresponding to the initial consonants of French *journal* (Polish *żurnal*) has a low functional yield. It can be identified by comparing *loge* (a French loan-word) and *load, rouge* and *rude, glazier* and *glacier, measure* and *mesher*, but the list of such pairs is not very extensive.

Musical aspects of language may have phonemic significance. In Mandarin Chinese of Pekin there are four pitches or tone levels which serve to distinguish words which would otherwise be homonyms: thus *chu* /ču/ pronounced on one tone means a pig; on another, bamboo; on another, lord or master; and on still another, to dwell. In many other languages the same situation is to be found. Even in English, where intonation usually plays a less decisive role in the determination of meaning, it may mark essential distinctions. The word "Ready?" spoken with rising intonation, stands for "Are you ready?" while the reply "Ready!" with falling intonation, stands for "Yes I am." The difference in musical inflexion is therefore phonemic. Differences in volume or stress may also be phonemic, as with English *'concert* (a noun) as opposed to *con'cert* (a verb). Finally, differences in length or quantity of a speech sound may have phonemic significance. A long vowel or consonant, marked in transcription with the sign [:], will in such cases contrast with a short one in two otherwise identical morphemes, as Spanish *pero* (but) as opposed to *perro* (dog) with the lengthened consonant [r:]. In Polish, contrasts in length of vowels are not phonemic. Here they may be called free variants.

3. Speech as a Continuum

We have been speaking about the units of human speech, the vowels and consonants, as if they were readily distinguishable in a stream of discourse. Actually this is not always so. Between major pauses there will be heard a stream of sound within which a listener ignorant of the language will find it at first difficult to isolate and identify separate phonemes. The difficulty will be increased by his natural tendency to detect the phonemic distinctions of his native language where they do not exist in the alien one, and conversely to ignore such essential distinctions in the latter if they do not exist in his own. Even the distinction between vowels and consonants, which a naive speaker may assume to be the same in all languages as in his own, is by no means a constant one, universally recognizable.

The stream of sound between major pauses is a continuum, so that physical boundaries between individual speech sounds (phonemes) are by no means sharply defined. Nevertheless there are recurrent pulses corresponding roughly to the emissions of breath from a speaker's lungs. Breath is most freely emitted in the speech sounds called vowels, where there is practically no friction encountered by air passing through the oral cavity (or the oral cavity and the nasal cavity combined, as in Polish q and $ę$). This is true of [i], [e], [u], [o] already noted in phonetic transcription, as well as others. By their nature vowels are conspicuous. Their presence marks a syllable constituting a unit of breath pulsation. Two vowel sounds articulated within a single syllable form a diphthong, for instance [ai]. It may be said that consonants, which are characterized by a constriction somewhere in the speech organs, are by nature attached to the conspicuous vowels, the readily identifiable nuclei of syllables. True enough: but what is a consonant in one language may be a vowel, or either a vowel or a consonant in another. The sounds represented in many alphabets by m, n, l and r involve a closure in the speech channel, and therefore qualify as consonants. But at the same time they have sufficiently "open" articulation to function as vowels or syllabic nuclei (German: *Silbenträger*) in some languages. When they thus function, the sounds are conventionally transcribed with a vertical mark beneath the characters: [m̩, n̩, l̩, r̩] to indicate that they are vocalic or syllabic consonants. In German the disyllabic word *Alpen* is often pronounced ['al-pm̩]; in English the word *table* is pronounced ['tei-bl̩]. In Czech a number of monosyllabic words rely on vocalic consonants as nuclei of syllables: *prst* (finger), *trn* (thorn), *vrch* (hill), *vrh* (a cast).

A syllable, then, is usually defined as a segment of speech consisting of a vowel (or vocalic consonant) with or without consonants attached to it. The simplest form is obviously a vowel alone, like the Polish conjunction *i* (and) or Icelandic *í* [i:] (in). But a syllable may be made up of a vowel flanked by clusters of consonants, as in the English word *strength* /streŋθ/. Here the effect is obviously much heavier than in the case of a syllable containing only a single consonant, like Polish *od* (from) or English *to*. In any event, the high point of the syllable is located in the vowel (or vocalic consonant) which owes its prominence to its open, unhindered articulation. Syllables may be readily counted from one peak to another. It is not always easy, however, to determine the boundaries between them, especially within those segments of an utterance such as groups of words which are uninterrupted by any perceptible pause. When a language like Japanese shows only syllables ending in vowels (open syllables, as they are called), the task of subdividing words into syllables is easy. Any consonant or group of consonants must be assigned to the beginning, thus constituting the syllable's initial boundary. But it is not so clear that the English verb *strengthen*, derived from the heavy monosyllable *strength*, should be divided in pronunciation into the two syllables *streng-then* /'streŋ-θn̩/ rather than *strength-en* /'streŋθ-n̩/, the more so since morphologically the word is clearly made up of two elements distinguishable according to the latter division: the nominal word-morpheme *strength* plus a suffix *-en* with a causative meaning. The verb *to strengthen* is semantically transparent in the sense of "to give strength; to cause to be strong." (Compare English *light*: *lighten*; *fat*: *fatten*, etc.)

In such cases syllabic units and morphological units frequently fail to coincide.

This lack of correspondence between phonology and morphology throws into relief another problem of speech analysis, namely the role of juncture or joining between a morpheme and what precedes or follows it. It is useful to distinguish three types of juncture (see ch. 3, sec. 5). Terminal juncture is in a sense negative, since it is really the absence of joining between morphemes. The clearest case is the silence occurring at the end of a complete utterance, or the pause occurring at the end of a sentence. Terminal juncture may also occur within a sentence. In either case it is comparable to a "rest" in musical notation. At the other extreme is closed juncture or absence of pause. Closed juncture means the joining of syllabic units without any breaks between them. Precisely because there may be no clearly defined boundary between syllables, the location of closed juncture within a stream of utterance is not always clear. Hence ambiguities may arise. The difference between English *nitrate* and *night-rate* is partly a matter of the incidence of junctures; in rapid speech the two can become indistinguishable. The meaning of a whole statement can be distorted when juncture is doubtful, as when "John scorns ale" is misunderstood "John's corns ail." In practical experience, such ambiguities are usually cleared up when a speaker is asked to repeat what he said. He will tend to do so at a slower tempo, and to introduce slight pauses and secondary stresses where none were previously perceptible. A slowed down tempo of speech will thus facilitate the identifying of closed junctures which are otherwise, it may be said, latent rather than apparent. (See p. 60f.)

Besides closed and terminal juncture there are various degrees of open juncture. Most commonly, but not always, open junctures correspond to the divisions between words. In written or printed discourse, conventional signs like spaces or hyphens are often used to indicate open junctures even where a word consists of a single consonant like Polish *w* or *z*. It should be stressed again that the situation differs from one language to another. In some the words of a sentence are so closely joined in sequence, that the final vowel or consonant of one will in many cases regularly affect the initial sound of the next following. In other languages words are not essentially affected in this way and the boundaries between them remain more distinct. Even then, however, it is not always easy to make a sharp division between open and closed juncture.

In analyzing a speech continuum for scientific purposes we do not have to rely entirely on subjective impressions. There is an instrument called the spectrograph which can record and photograph the complex series of vibrations of the air which convey a sequence of spoken sounds. The basic tone or basic frequency of vibration of any vowel, for instance, may be chosen at will, but what makes it identifiable for the listener will be the frequencies and relations of the overtones or higher vibrations which are characteristic for that vowel, and that one alone. These for their part are determined by the position and functioning of the speech organs and the shape of the aperture through which a stream of air is emitted in the act of enunciation. The consonants are less clearly registered, for obvious reasons. Many of them have very brief moments of articulation as compared with vowels.

4. GENERAL TRENDS IN SOUND PATTERNS

When we have at our disposal sufficient written records for a single language or language group, covering a period of a millenium or more, we are often able to deduce some consistent, orderly transformations in the system of sounds (or, more accurately, in the system of significant sound contrasts). Such changes are general, not obviously dependent on phonetic environments.

For example, the records of English lead us to deduce a general tendency, beginning in the late 14th and early 15th centuries, to raise the vowels from a position of lower articulation to a higher. Thus long $\bar{e}$ [e:] became [i:] and $\bar{o}$ [o:] became [u:], while original $\bar{\imath}$ [i:] and $\bar{u}$ [u:] began to diphthongize. This happened in all positions: that is, regardless of phonetic environment. The words $b\bar{o}k$ and $t\bar{o}th$ and $g\bar{o}d$, ancestors of modern book, tooth and good, illustrate the trend of [o:] in differing environments. The vowels with lower articulation followed the upward trend somewhat later.

Another general trend could be pointed out in Polish, namely the marked tendency towards the palatalization of consonants. Other Slavic languages show the same trend, but to a less degree.

Sometimes the reason for a general trend may be found in the internal structure of a phonemic system. It has been pointed out that such systems are usually symmetrical. That is to say, if there is a complete set of voiceless stop consonants *p t k* in a given language, it will usually be found to correspond to a complete set of voiced stops *b d g*, or to none at all. There are in fact languages which have a complete repertory of the voiceless stops but lack all voiced stops. Thus they are still symmetrical, but they would not be if they had, let us say, *b* alone but not *d* or *g*. In such a situation there would be an imbalance of the phonemic pattern, and this might well favour the change of *b* to something else.

One example from the history of English may suffice. In the period called Late Old English, antedating 1066, there had existed a genuine phonemic contrast between the unrounded front vowel *i* whether long or short, and the rounded one *y* (corresponding to modern German *ü*), whether long or short. This distinction kept apart such morpheme pairs as the roots of the verbs *till-an* meaning to aim at something and *for-tyll-an* meaning to seduce. But by this time *y* was the only vowel of its type in the system. It was therefore in a sense in a weak position because of lack of contrast with analogous (non-existent) rounded vowels. Hence we are not surprised to observe that it was eliminated from the system by being transformed into *i* in all positions. The new *i*'s and the original ones thus fell together. The result was of course a multiplication of homonymous morphemes; but such an eventuality does not seem to act as a deterrent to a general sound change affecting a phonemic system.

It can likewise be established that the changes affecting the system of early Germanic consonants (see ch. 1, sec. 4) occurred in such a way, by successive stages, as to preserve a symmetry of contrasts. But the first impulse towards the general consonant shift—the transformation of [p, t, k] into [f, θ, χ]—remains something of a mystery. Such basic changes were, as far as we know, not conditioned by neighbouring sounds. This does not mean that they were "unconditioned" in the sense of being causeless, but that the cause is not known to us. There is no doubt here as to which sounds are the older. They are the ones preserved in the great majority of the Indo-European linguistic families, including those, like Indo-Iranian, Hellenic and Italic, with the oldest written records.

Extra-linguistic factors such as climate or social organization have sometimes been suggested as causes of so-called "unconditioned" sound changes. Such attempted explanations are highly speculative and should be regarded with great caution. The same may be said of attempts to explain why the tempo of change differs from language to language. Modern Icelandic, as we have said, is very conservative as compared to closely related Swedish, Norwegian or Danish. All of these are descended from Old Scandinavian. But Icelandic alone has preserved, among others, the initial [θ]-sound just mentioned. It has been thought by some that the geographical isolation of Icelanders, separated from their fellow Scandinavians and living on a distant island, might explain the archaism of their speech. But the opposite is true of Polynesian languages to be found on remote islands of the Pacific Ocean. Here the sound changes must have occurred more rapidly than in the conservative Indonesian group (including Malayan on the mainland peninsula). This does not mean, of course, that the events of external history such as emigrations, conquest, and various forms of cultural contacts may not have a decisive influence on the course of a language. Its accentuation, intonation and phonetic system may be affected by a neighbour. But here we are dealing with specifically linguistic factors once more. When both languages are known—the one influenced and the one exercising an influence upon it—it is possible to describe accurately the causes of changes occurring in the former. When one of them is lost, as was the prehistoric language of ancient Ireland at the time of the Celtic invasion, we can only guess about the nature of its possible effect on the surviving one.

A general tendency towards specific change, such as the consistent raising of vowels in early Modern English from lower positions to higher, or the general shift of consonants in early Germanic, has been designated as linguistic "drift" by the American scholar Edward Sapir. The term is a metaphor for presumably inherent trends comparable to the current of a river. As metaphor, it does not well fit the purposes of scientific description. Some trends which may on the surface appear to be arbitrary, such as the loss of final unaccented vowels in late Old French and Middle English, can sometimes be tied up with factors of prosody which are not clearly indicated in written texts. Much work remains to be done in an effort to define the conditions under which general sound changes occur.

Whatever the reasons for general sound changes, whether apparent or not, they occur gradually. This must be so, else members of one generation would have difficulty in understanding those of another. We also know that sound changes (no matter how regular) within a given language or family of languages, operate over a definable historical period, and then cease to operate. At a certain time the speakers of a hypothetical language which we call Early Germanic shifted the pronunciation of original [t] to [θ], as we have seen in the discussion of English *three* when compared with its Latin cognate *trēs*. But later on the trend towards such a shift no longer operated. Words beginning with a *t-*, when borrowed from a foreign language at a later date, did not undergo such a change, as we see from the English word *tone* derived from Latin *tonus* by way of the French. Its first consonant has not been transformed into anything like [θ]. In the same way Polish *teleologia*, a late loan-word, has an unchanged initial *t* in front of a front vowel, whereas Polish shows palatalization of the initial *t* in original Slavic words.

Here we see evidence that sound changes are limited in time. They are also limited geographically. Within the confines of a single fairly unified language there will be found variations of dialectal pronunciation definable by districts. All of this means simply that "sound laws" do not exist in the same sense that laws of physics exist, independent of time and place. At most we can speak of regular changes in pronunciation occurring consistently over a given area within a given period of time. The regularity is often such that, granted a sufficient number of examples of cognate words taken from related languages and their dialects, scholars are able to surmise with considerable assurance what were the forms in a lost "parent" language from which the cognates were derived. The words for the number three in extant Indo-European languages (see above) show very many regular correspondences with other words containing an analogous sequence of phonemes, and the words are obviously related among themselves, both in phonetic pattern and in meaning. A mere glance at the forms: Sanskrit *tráyas*, Greek τρεῖς *treîs* (the circumflex accent indicating pronunciation due to contraction of syllables), Latin *trēs* (with long vowel), Old Slavic *trьje* and Gothic *preis*, etc., would suggest that all of them were descended from a lost form, the common ancestor of all: something like *trejes* (that is, *treies* pronounced as two syllables, not three).

A form like **trejes* is, as we say, reconstructed. We have excellent reasons for supposing that a word like this was spoken in prehistoric times by a people whose speech eventually gave rise (by emigration? transfer? internal changes? contact with other peoples?) to the Indo-European languages as we know them. Yet it is important to remember, as the distinguished French scholar Antoine Meillet frequently emphasized, that all such reconstructed starred forms represent merely a formula of systematic correspondences among extant forms. They should not be confused with words known to us by written or spoken records. Sometimes it happens that our previous image of a reconstructed form has to be modified in the light of new knowledge. The decipherment of Hittite, an early cognate or offshoot of Indo-European (scholars disagree as to the exact relationship) yielded evidence for the existence of no less than four special consonants called laryngeals which were not allowed for in 19th-century reconstructions of the parent language. Their existence at some early stage helps to explain, among other things, the alternation of long and short vowels in cognate Indo-European words. The recent decipherment of inscriptions found on the island of Crete and dating from about 1400 B.C. contributes towards a new, modified picture of prehistoric Greek, which developed into a number of known dialects in historical times: Attic, Ionian, Doric, Boeetian, etc. Such corrective discoveries are a reminder of the tentative nature of all reconstructions.

5. SOME TYPES OF SOUND CHANGE

It was pointed out in the preceding section that consonants are sometimes palatalized, that is, shifted towards pronunciation on the palate rather than elsewhere in the mouth: i.e., with the tongue raised towards the palate. Again one may cite Polish *cicho* /čiχo/ as opposed to Russian *muxo* /tiχo/, with the former showing a shift from the teeth towards the palate. Or the Modern Italian pronunciation of *circo* with initial /č/ instead of the /k/ of the classical Latin *circum*. In both, the articulation of the initial consonant has been approximated more closely to the place of articulation of the coming vowel. In general terms, two sounds have been made more similar than they were before.

Assimilation is the term applied to this general process. Sometimes it results in complete identity of the two previously unlike sounds. The word *assimilation* itself comes from a verb **ad-similāre* having a prefix meaning to or towards, still fully preserved in words like *advise, administer*. Modern Italian is particularly rich in examples of assimilation, as may be seen by comparing *retto* with its ancestor *rectō, trasformare* with *transformāre, sogetto* (the *g* here representing the palatal combination [dʒ] with *subjectō*). Here the spelling with doubled consonants actually indicates a prolonged or "doubled" sound comparable to that in the English *book-case*. The lengthened consonant thus preserves a quantitative trace of the one earlier lost by assimilation. In other languages the result is not only a single sound but a short one: the first of the two consonants is in the end completely lost. Polish spelling of the word *asymilacja* indicates such a final result, while the English spelling *assimilation*, with its double *s*, reflects an antecedent stage.

Complete assimilation can occur, by the way, between consonants not standing in immediate juxtaposition, as when the word for five in Indo-European, something like *penkwe*, developed in Latin into *quinque*.

Partial assimilation results in approximation short of complete identity. The Latin negative prefix *in-*, preserved in its unmodified form before morphemes beginning with a vowel (compare *inaudible, inoperative*), is changed to *im-* before those beginning with a consonant made with the lips, as in *impossible*. The voicing of previously voiceless consonants in the neighbourhood of voiced sounds, whether vowels or consonants, is a type of partial assimilation often encountered: compare Spanish *vida* derived from Latin *vita*, as already cited; also Polish *egzamin* derived from Latin *exāmen*, where *x* stands for [ks].[1] Sometimes the transformation is a matter of vowel assimilation: two vowels originally of unlike articulation are brought closer together or even made identical because of proximity. Prehistoric Latin had a form *semilis*, known to us as *similis*. Prehistoric Germanic had a form *maniz* which produced German *Männer*, English *men*. In both cases the vowel has been raised to a higher position because there was once a high front vowel in the second syllable. For Germanic languages this sort of vowel assimilation is known as umlaut. But the phenomenon is by no means limited to one time or place. Isolated instances can be heard in popular speech, as when the Latin *Geminī* (meaning twin gods) is transformed into *Jimini*, or when *etch-*

---

[1] It should be recalled that the incidence of accent may play a part in deciding whether the voicing—that is, partial assimilation to voiced environment—is to occur. The words *exāmen* and *egzamin* have stress on the second syllable. The first syllables, spoken with less emphasis, were therefore more prone to voicing. But the Latin prefix *ex-* [eks] was accented on the first syllable in words like *extra*. Therefore Polish has *ekstra* and English has *extra* pronounced with [ks], without partial assimilation to the voiced (vocalic) environment. The alternation of voiceless and voiced consonants depending chiefly on environment and incidence of accent, is very familiar in early Germanic languages. The systematic alternation of the two types under these conditions is summarized as Verner's Law, named from the Danish scholar who first called attention to the existence of this correlation. (See ch. 1, sec. 4.)

ings is transformed by an individual lapse of the tongue into *itchings*.

Anticipation is the most general term which can be applied to all types of assimilation mentioned so far, because the speaker in every case modifies his pronunciation in view of a coming sound. Something being said is affected by something not yet said. From the point of view of acoustics, a branch of physics, such a statement would of course be absurd. In this realm a nonexistent factor cannot be said to affect one already existent. But from the point of view of psychology, such a statement has meaning. Human beings look ahead to coming events, whether consciously or unconsciously. Because of long-familiar habits they may adjust their speech organs in conformity to the requirements of a sound expected to come but not yet enunciated. In this sense, then, the causal relations in human linguistic behaviour differ from those which obtain in physics.

Deferred or delayed influences, where sounds already spoken affect those to come, result in what is called progressive assimilation. They are actually less common than the anticipatory ones. Under these we might classify patterns of vowel harmony in the Finno-Ugric languages, where the first vowel of a polysyllabic word determines the quality of vowels in the syllables to come including suffixed endings. When a consonant changes into a vowel, its nature may be determined by the sound preceding it. Thus in early English a combination of the two phonemes /χt/ became /jt/ or /wt/, eventually /it/ or /ut/, depending on whether the preceding vowel was a front one like *e* or a back one like *o*. The forward-operating influence of the original vowels has helped to produce two different kinds of diphthongs, as can be seen by comparing modern English *light* (from *le(o)ht*) with *thought* (from *thōht*). In the first case the *h* developed into an *i*, in the second into an *u*. Similarly, the final consonant of English verbs like *sleep*, *lead* determines in advance whether the affixed morpheme for the third person singular inflection of the present tense is to be voiceless or voiced: [s] for *sleep*, [z] for *lead*.

Assimilation, whether partial or complete, progressive or regressive, may be compared with an opposite kind of conditioned sound change.

Dissimilation, as the term implies, is a change which causes two sounds to become less alike than they were previously. A series of identical or very similar sounds coming in close proximity will cause difficulties, as any school-child knows from practising such "tongue twisters" as "she sells sea shells." In single words, the nasals *m, n* and the liquids *r, l* (as they are sometimes called) are particularly troublesome when they appear in clusters. One way of reducing the element of excessive similarity is to drop one of the consonants in question, as when Latin *flēbilis*, meaning deplorable and hence weak, was transformed into French *faible*, English *feeble*. In Spanish the name *Frederick* appears as *Federico*; in Italian the Latin *propriō* has yielded *propio*. Sometimes too a repetition of like syllables is avoided by omission of one of them, as when Latin *nutritrix* was simplified to *nutrix*, ancestor of English *nurse*. Another way of avoiding repetition is to change one of the consonants into another one of like but not identical articulation. An ancient Greek word πορφύρα (whence the English loan-word from the adjectival *porphyry*) was taken over in Latin as *purpura*. Later it was dissimilated and passed through French into English as *purple*. Old French had a word *alme* from Latin *anima*, meaning soul. The Latin *corridor*, when borrowed into Russian, was transformed into *kolidor*. A third method of diversifying a cluster of like consonants is to introduce a new one that varies from them in some ways while at the same time retaining some similarity in articulation with the others. Latin *numerus*, current in popular speech as something like **num'ro* or **num'rum*, appears in French as *nombre* (English *number*). English *timber*, shows the same dissimilation as compared with Dutch *timmer*, German *Zimmer*. Finally, a combination of the second and third types of dissimilation is also possible: one of two similar consonants may be changed, and at the same time a third may be introduced. Hence Spanish *hombre* from Latin *homine* (a form of *homo*, meaning man). The second nasal became a liquid, and the voiced labial stop was inserted between them, thus completing the diversification. The same process, with change of initial *f-* into *h-* (now unpronounced) produced Spanish *hambre* meaning hunger, corresponding to *famine* in English (a loan-word ultimately from the Latin).

Interchange of two sounds is apt to occur, especially when they are similarly articulated. The technical name for this is metathesis. Again, liquids and nasals are most subject to this change. For this reason we find German *brennen* beside English *burn*, modern English *bird* beside Middle English *brid*, and many others.

Individual lapses in colloquial speech often exemplify some of the sound changes here discussed. In English, when someone says *orchresta* for *orchestra* he is anticipating the enunciation of a consonant; when he says *mineral* instead of *minimal* he is dissimilating a series of nasals; when he says *plotoprasm* for *protoplasm* he is exemplifying metathesis. (Compare the popular Polish *ulegurować* for *uregulować*, meaning to regulate.) When he says *wordly* for *worldly* he is dissimilating by omitting one of two identical consonants. When he pronounces *due* like *jew* he is palatalizing a consonant not usually palatalized; when he says *lemme* for *let me* he is completely assimilating two different consonants.

Such individual lapses or aberrations usually remain without effect. They are sometimes corrected by the speaker himself, often ignored by both speaker and listener. But in certain periods in the history of individual languages, such lapses or aberrations must have gained wide currency, otherwise we could not explain their ultimate general acceptance, causing a readjustment in the distribution of phonemes. Sound changes of wider scope—those sometimes called unconditioned, like the early Germanic sound shift—must also have begun with transitional periods when first a minority, then a majority, then all speakers of a given community adopted the newer pronunciation.

Why it is that minority lapses or aberrations sometimes prevail and sometimes do not, is not as yet explained. The question is part of the general problem concerning the possible relation of linguistic to extra-linguistic factors. Sometimes we can see that changes represented by individual lapses are accepted or not accepted in a speech community according as they fit into a general trend, or into the maintenance of symmetry in the pattern of phonemic relations. Sometimes the trend results in a conservation of speech energy, as when consonants become vowels in the neighbourhood of vowels. But the opposite may also be true, as when the vowel -*u* in Greek diphthongs developed into /v/ (compare the present-day Russian pronunciation of the borrowed prefix *eu*- as *jev* in such names as *Eugene* and *Europe*; it reflects the medieval Greek pronunciation, still preserved). Once again we must conclude that more information is needed before we can attempt to codify the reasons for sound changes, whether they lie in well-known habits of pronunciation, widely attested and frequently observed, or in extra-linguistic factors.

CHAPTER 6

THE STRUCTURE OF A LANGUAGE

1. MAJOR UNITS OF UTTERANCE: WHAT IS A SENTENCE?

The individual sounds of specific languages (the phonemes) are, as we have seen, combined in units called morphemes. The morphemes may constitute words (whatever "word" may mean) or they may be parts of words. The question now arises: How are words put together to make up major units of utterances?

The expression "major units of utterances" is rather vague, and deliberately so. Traditional grammars deal with sentences, major and minor parts of sentences, and sentence-equivalents. But the definitions given have often been unsatisfactory. Old-fashioned grammars of English offered such definitions as this: "A sentence is a group of words expressing a complete thought." Obviously, it would be very difficult to determine what constitutes a complete thought, whether by tests of logic or philosophy or language alone. But fortunately we can apply some tests of a more objective character than this when it comes to the dividing of a stream of utterances into its major parts.

Spoken language is realized in units of widely varying length, from the sustained discourses of an orator to the short utterances making up a rapid conversation. This is true in human communities of all sorts, including those which as yet lack writing. It is important indeed to take spoken discourse as our point of departure in this as in other problems of linguistic analysis.

A sustained discourse may be a story told for the information or entertainment of listeners, or a speech delivered to persuade them towards some line of action. A stranger approaching the group of listeners from a distance may at first hear nothing but a stream of sounds. Later, on coming closer, he will notice pauses of longer and shorter duration. At the beginning and end there is silence. The pauses obviously subdivide the discourse into units of some sort. Each pause, it will be observed, is typically preceded by one or another of a limited group of intonation patterns, or of certain phoneme sequences often repeated, or a gesture (or a combination of some of these) which can be identified even by someone who does not know the language. The impressions will be very general, of course, but they will give the first indications about the major units into which the long speech is to be subdivided.

A stranger listening to an informal conversation in an alien tongue will be able to identify the same sort of acoustic signals, probably more frequently used. If the interchange is made up of short utterances, the pre-pause signals may occur at the end of each one. (See pp. 61 and 101 on juncture.)

But here and there they may be lacking. The listener, if he has come to rely on his identification of signals, would then have reason to be puzzled. Why no indication of a coming pause? But if he possesses even a rudimentary knowledge of the language, he will notice that on such occasions the listener responds with an enquiry to this effect: "What were you about to say?" (Parenthetically it may be remarked that questions as well as statements have their own pre-pause signals in various languages: sometimes the same, sometimes different.) This means that the pause was here misleading, and has confused the listener. In popular terms, it left him uncertain as to the speaker's meaning or intention. The inquiry informs us (if we understand it) that a unit of discourse was interrupted: whether by external or internal (psychological) causes is unimportant.

In other words, there is a difference between a normal, planned pause and an accidental one due to interruption. Here we have a clue to the definition of the basic units of discourse, popularly known as sentences. The basic units are marked off by pauses or silences, often reinforced by other signals, initial or final. Of course the pauses may be of unequal importance and duration, and the signals of unequal prominence. In some situations a speaker reinforces a coming pause or a silence by some such expression as "I have finished" (compare Polish *Skończyłem*). Others are less clear. But the units can be identified by means often facilitated by appeal to the usage of native speakers: that is, by asking them "Would you say this?"—"... or that?" Also by asking: "Have you finished?" or words to that effect. The answers to such questions can be arrived at by more roundabout means, to be sure, relying less on the pronouncements of naive, untutored speakers. But in any event it is possible to formulate tests for basic units of discourse recognized as complete by listeners to them.

Such units may be single words. "Yesterday" is a complete statement in response to the question "When did you arrive?" It would not, however, be a complete statement if a speaker enunciated the word "Yesterday," spoken in such a way as to presuppose further utterances, and then abruptly broke off, as if he were about to say "Yesterday I arrived," but did not finish. On the other hand the units may be fairly long and will be so understood by the listener if he is kept waiting for the signals—initial or final or both—which serve to mark them off.

In written (printed) languages such signals are usually made visual. Punctuation indicates by a period (as for instance in "Yesterday.") that an utterance is supposed to be a complete unit. It indicates by a dash (as for instance in "Yesterday—") that it is incomplete. These well-known aids to the interpretation of written characters are very valuable, but they are not quite sufficient for European languages, and surely not adequate for many others. In many instances an indication of tones and intonation curves is required, and conventional punctuation does not provide this fully.

In languages as spoken, the signals do provide a means of blocking off units of discourse into what we may call sentences. Let us state, provisionally, that a sentence is an utterance which satisfies certain norms of completeness in a given language. The norms are to be recognized in various ways, depending on the language being described. Patterns of intonation (as in English) represent one type of norm very commonly employed.

Within the units thus distinguished there may be minor units. If a sentence is made up of a single word like "Yesterday" it is as such indivisible, but if it is made up of a number of words as in

"Yesterday I gave this book to Professor Smith," it may be sub-divided into groups of words constituting the sentence elements. Such subdivision is made possible by the recognition of various signals, including junctures as well as others. The problem of subdividing sentences and analyzing them into their parts may be called the problem of identifying immediate constituents (IC's, as the term is sometimes abbreviated) and ultimate or individual constituents (in many languages identical with morphemes, as defined in chapter 3). In any case such analysis leads to a very fundamental question concerning the functioning of words and groups of words in sentences.

2. THE SO-CALLED PARTS OF SPEECH AND THEIR INFLEXIONS

In some languages, but by no means all, it should be remembered, individual words are subject to morphological changes. These may be expressed by means of modified prefixes, infixes and suffixes (including zero elements or absence of such affixes). The phenom-enon will be very familiar to anyone who has studied Latin or Greek, or who speaks a modern inflected language such as German or any of the Slavic tongues. Let us take Latin as an example. Here we find sentences such as *Dominus venīt* (meaning "The master came") and *Dominus vīcit* (meaning "The master has conquered") but also *Dominō dedī* ("I gave it to the master") and *Dominum vīdī* ("I saw the master"). Clearly we have to do with a single word meaning master or lord, which is subject to change according to its use in a sentence. The inflexion is realized by means of morphemes which are bound forms affixed to an identical root. In such a situation we are clearly not dealing with word-for-mation or the creation of new words, but of modifications affecting one and the same word.

Examination of a sufficient number of texts will eventually yield a full inventory of modified forms assumed by a root like *domin-*. It will also show that many other words have the same inventory so far as their endings are concerned. In other terms it can be said that a general, inflexional pattern has been established for words of a certain class which for the time being may be left nameless, or referred to by a colourless numeral as Class I. By the same method other patterns may be recognized which, while showing some points of similarity with the first (e.g. a form *dominā-m* compared with *dominu-m*), nevertheless are clearly distinct and separate. These may be considered members of a related Class II. The process is simpler if the investigator is dealing with a dead language like Latin, preserved in a fixed number of unchanging inscriptions and written records; it is more difficult if he is dealing with a previously unknown language lacking such records. In any event it may be expected that additional classes of patterns may emerge if one class is already found that is marked by multiple endings appearing in subclasses or variant forms.

In a highly inflected language, then, like Latin or the modern Slavic tongues, classes may be recognized by indubitable external signs. Sometimes it will be found that a given inflected form is frequently located in close proximity to another non-inflected one, as for instance the Latin short free forms *in, ab, ad, pro* (themselves uninflected) are regularly followed by words showing a very restricted number of endings. Position in relation to other forms may, that is to say, have something to do with the appearance of specific inflected forms rather than others in the stream of discourse. It should be remembered, of course, that inflexion is by no means limited to the adding of suffixes at the end of a word. There are languages which use patterns of prefixes instead, and internal changes (infixes, changes of consonants or of vowels) are not uncommon. Very familiar is the internal vowel change represented in English *sing* : *sang, drive* : *drove.* (See ch. 3, sec. 2.)

By various clues such as similar modification of form, juxtaposition and other types of set word order, it is often possible to establish classes of words which are known as parts of speech. A classification and a terminology to be used in describing these categories was worked out by the Greeks for their own language, and taken over by the Romans. In the Latinized form it became widely adapted for usage in describing modern European languages, even where it was not readily applicable. Moreover, it was often extended to the description of very different languages, where the categories indicated by Graeco-Latin terminology simply do not exist.[1] Basically the problem is one of finding a terminology which will be descriptive without being either misleading or else metaphorical.

Fundamentally, the classification of words (whether inflected or not) into parts of speech depends on their use in sentences, sometimes taken in combination with the forms they assume. But no classification can be entirely rigid, even where elaborate inflexions offer abundant objective evidence. Overlappings and ambiguities occur even in clearly patterned languages.

It has been said more than once[2] that all sentences consist of two basic elements: something mentioned, and something said about it. At first sight this may not appear to be true of many utterances defined as complete sentences in the preceding section, for instance the expression "Yesterday" in answer to a question. Here however the situation is clarified when the linguistic context is carefully examined. The enunciation "Yesterday" with sentence-final intonation shows that the word depends on a preceding question such as "When did you arrive?" In the same way the single Polish word *Jemu* (To him) may be the complete reply to a question "To

---

[1] Implicit in some of the Greek terms were occasional metaphors which could lead to misunderstanding. The word πτῶσις (*ptōsis*) was applied by Aristotle to inflected forms of words as compared with a form considered basic, such as the "nominative" of nouns. Literally this means a falling. Translated, it became Latin *cāsus*, also a falling; compare German *Fall* and Polish *przypadek*, modelled on the Latin. The fourth case, as it is often called in Polish, was called πτῶσις αἰτιατική (*ptōsis aitiātikē*), which might mean "case of accusing" as well as "case pertaining to that which is caused or effected." The Romans translated it as *accusativus*. The meaning implied is lively, but much too restricted. (See Jespersen, *Language*, p. 20.)

[2] For instance, Hermann Paul, *Prinzipien der Sprachgeschichte*, 4th ed. (Halle a/S., 1909), p. 124; Edward Sapir, *Language* (New York, 1921), ch. 5. Sapir's discussion is based on a knowledge of very many languages spoken in many parts of the world. He concludes that some method is needed in all of them to show the relationship between a thing and an action. Thing and action are of course to be understood in a very broad sense. The former may include abstractions, and the latter, expressions for mere states of being.

whom did you give it?" The context of discourse thus sometimes affords the missing elements required for a formally complete sentence embodying the two essential elements mentioned. In actual conversation, "Yesterday" will be understood to mean "I arrived yesterday," and "Jemu" to mean "Jemu dałem." We are justified therefore in extending the elliptical replies if, and only if, the conversational context warrants it. In other circumstances the single words *yesterday* and *jemu*, spoken out of context, would elicit questions like "What do you mean? What about it?"—and so on. The general linguistic situation may be essential in establishing relations of spoken elements with others previously spoken and therefore implicitly carried over even if not expressed. There are situations where the statement about something refers to its existence merely, whether directly or indirectly, as in stage directions, labels on buildings or announcements like "A ship!" or "High tide."[3]

It should be parenthetically stressed that not all languages conform equally clearly to the sentence structure subject + predicate. The Totonac Indians of East-central Mexico have developed a highly synthetic one-word sentence core (verbal or nominal) which constitutes an utterance complete in itself without the bipartite division found in most languages.[4]

Assuming that these two fundamental elements can be deduced however expressed, the question is: how are words related to them? By form or position, or by both, they usually make up or are attached to one or the other. According to traditional categories in Indo-European grammars, nouns and verbs, recognizable in some instances primarily by inflexion (e.g. Slavic languages) and in some by position primarily though supplemented by inflexion (e.g. English, Dutch, French), represent the two groups of capital importance because they are directly related to the basic purposes

---

[3] In English such statements, which have intonation marking completeness, are sometimes called presentations or presentative sentences.

[4] See Norman A. McQuown, "Analysis of the Cultural Content of Language Materials," *Language in Culture*, ed. Harry Hoijer (University of Chicago, 1954), p. 29.

of speech. A noun, it is generally understood, is the name (Latin *nōmen*) of something; a verb refers to an action or a condition.[5] The definition is at best approximate if not actually misleading, as is apparent in view of the "verbal nouns," so-called, which exist in many languages. Other parts of speech traditionally designated are: adjectives (qualifiers in a general sense, primarily of nouns), adverbs (qualifiers also, primarily of verbs), and prepositions (a class of words with the function of standing before other words, and thus signalizing something about the latters' relationship with still other words in a sentence). Here too the terminology is misleading: adverbs are found in practice to qualify non-verbs, and prepositions may on occasion stand after the words signalized; compare Latin *vōbis-cum* beside *cum vōbis*, English "across the fields" with archaic "the fields across." Moreover, there are borderline cases in many Indo-European languages where single words appear to function in a dual or ambiguous capacity. Compare English "He climbed up" with "He climbed up the hill"; Latin *Dei gratia* in the sense of "by God's grace" with the same expression in *caret Dei gratia* meaning "He lacks God's grace." In the one case English *up* is clearly tied up with the verb while in the other it is tied up with the following noun as well. So the Latin *gratia* is in one case tied up directly with *Dei* but in the other with the verb *caret* as well. Less ambiguous is the term pronoun applied to a word that stands for a noun. Here the function defining the part of speech concerned may be tested by a simple technique of substituting. When someone says "He came," the response may be "Who came?" and the reply: "The carpenter came." Thus there is no doubt about the function of *he*.

If the parts of speech are not definable with logical strictness in the Indo-European languages, the same may be said of the inflexional forms under which they appear. Nouns, for instance, are said to have gender, which is widely interpreted as something having to do with sex. This is because a considerable number of

---

[5] The Latin *verbum* had a wider meaning as well, standing for a word of any sort. So did the Greek ῥῆμα (*rhēma*), meaning a discourse, that which said.

nouns in Latin and Greek (but by no means all, or even a majority) which shared common inflexional endings were found to refer to biological creatures of the female sex. The same was found true of other nouns with common inflexional endings, many of which referred to creatures of the masculine sex. Yet very many examples indicate that other nouns fall into categories having nothing to do with biology.

Verbs, supposed to concern themselves with action and states of being, are said to have tenses. The word tense in English is derived from Latin *tempus* by way of French *temps*; the historically attested meaning is time (compare Polish *czas*). But grammatical tenses cannot be neatly coordinated with divisions of time. A few examples will suffice to demonstrate this. In English the verb form *comes* is usually employed to indicate present time, but in certain contexts it may indicate future time ("When he comes, I'll see him" or "If he comes, I'll see him"). In Polish as in other Slavic languages the nature or "aspect" of an action (whether continuous, instantaneous, or already concluded) is expressed by inflexion, as well as its time of realization: *z-rob-ił* means not only "he did it in the past" but "he did it in the past once and for all and finished it"; *z-rob-i* means "he will do it in the future and finish it"; *rob-i* means "he is doing it now and has not finished it," while *rob-ił* means "he was doing it in the past, repeatedly, or without having finished it." Notice that in the first two instances the prefix *z-* is associated with two different times but only one aspect, sometimes known as the perfective or completed. The absence of *z-* is associated with one aspect only but (depending on the suffix) with two different times. In other words, there is here an overlapping of categories as formulated in traditional grammar. Another instructive example of overlapping categories will be found in Polish verbal nouns. These are not only derived from verbal roots—a procedure paralleled in many languages of many types—but besides being subject to nominal declension they also indicate verbal aspect (that is completed versus incompleted action) and may even take an object: *możliwość spotkania się* in the sense of "the possibility of meeting once" (genitive case, perfective aspect, followed by reflexive pronoun object) and *możliwość spotykania się* (the same construction in continuous aspect, meaning the possibility of repeated meetings).

3. DESCRIBING PARTS OF SPEECH

All of this does not mean that it is futile to classify the words or lexical units of a language according to classes, depending on form, position and function. But it does mean that traditional terminology is sometimes misleading. Revisions have been proposed: sometimes the substitution of new terms for ambiguous old ones, sometimes the complete elimination of all old ones and their replacement by an algebraic system of numbers and letters. The latter device (which has not yet been worked out with entire consistency) might well eliminate the most serious dangers of ambiguity, but at the expense of any correlation between form and meaning.[6] Externally dissimilar forms would still have to be grouped together and designated under identical rubrics, no matter how neutral the terminology, and this fact itself implies a certain correlation. The basic reason for it is connected with syntax (see below).

It is important, as we have seen, to be on one's guard about the application of classical terminology to modern Indo-European languages. The warning is even more pertinent when it comes to the terminology to be applied to non-Indo-European languages.

Categories of time and mode of action (finished and unfinished; possible, impossible or probable, etc.) are for us habitually associated with the parts of speech we call verbs. But other languages make other associations. In Japanese, for instance, both verbs and adjectives are used as predicative words (that is, words which serve to assert something about something; the second of the two essential functions of discourse as previously indicated). This is basically true of other languages in which no verb meaning to be or to exist need be expressed between a noun and an attributive adjective, as in Hebrew and Russian. But in Japanese, adjectives

---

[6] Such a system of algebraic references by number and letter has been worked out by Charles C. Fries in his *Structure of English* (New York, 1952).

also express modes of being or action such as imperfective and perfective (continuous or incompleted versus completed) which we are accustomed to associate with verbs. Why not? The quality or characteristic expressed by an adjective may be subject to change. In Mende, a Bantu language of Africa, pronouns as well as verbs express time relationship: the I who does something now is not the same person who did it in the past. Again—why not? Here the doer of an action is recognized as subject to change, not merely the time or aspect of the action itself. In such cases it is clearly important to create terms for inflexional variations which will give a clue to their meaning (function, if you will) as well as their form. Or at least to the correlation of forms among themselves (a matter of syntax) which itself implies meaning. Yet the terms should be sufficiently broad and inclusive, in order not to be misleading.

We are accustomed to designate as prepositions and conjunctions certain groups of words in the Indo-European languages having the sole function of expressing relations between other words and groups of words in a sentence, while lacking readily defined meanings of their own. For this reason they are sometimes referred to in a general way as "empty" words or function words. Certainly when taken alone, out of any context, such words as *on* and *if* and *but* are more difficult to define lexically than such words as *head* or *give*. Their linguistic function, as well as their lack of distinct correlatives in the objective world of things and events, would seem to mark them off in a distinct category. Yet there are languages in which these functional word-classes are far less readily distinguished than in ours. In Ewe, a West-African language, the word *dzi* has a wide range of meanings, including: sky, surface, upwards, on top, above, towards, pertaining to. When used as an "empty" or relational word it is post-positional: *élètɔdzí*[7] means "he is on the water (literally: the water on)." *Me*,

---

[7] In Ewe, there are five tones with phonemic significance. The acute and grave accents indicate high and low tones respectively; lack of accent on an initial syllable means low tone. The phonetic character [ɔ] stands for a vowel like that in English *taught*.

a noun (as we understand the term), meaning a place inside another, may also mean extension of time or space, and also during, to, on, near, under and between, while ŋgɔ meaning front or front part, may similarly mean before in the sense of time as well as place ("I stood before the house" as well as "He was chief before me"). Thus, concrete terms for objects in space serve to express relations of time as well as space, and even more abstract relations such as causation (*post hoc ergo propter hoc!*).

But such shifting or elasticity of category is not by any means limited to languages like Ewe which lack overt signs such as inflexion to mark nouns off from prepositions, postpositions, or other parts of speech. A shifting of categories can be observed still in process or but recently accomplished in inflected Indo-European languages today. In Modern Irish, the conjunction *when* is expressed by *'n uair*, where *uair* (from Latin *hora*) by itself stands for hour, time or weather; thus literally "the time that"; the German prepositions *statt* and *wegen* are specialized forms of nouns meaning place and ways (compare English *instead* meaning in place of). The very abstract English adversative conjunction *but*, meaning nevertheless, has been contracted from a phrase *be ūtan* meaning by the outside (of something). The conjunction *until, till* is developed from a noun meaning aim (compare the cognate German *Ziel* meaning goal). This process of transition from concrete to "empty" function-word may be observed in such contemporary English locutions as this: "Directly you reach London, you must ring him up." The first word is according to form an adverb, as the *-ly* suffix indicates; according to its lexical history it originally applied to spatial relations. Yet here it is clearly a substitute for the temporal conjunction *when* or *as soon as*. Similarly the concrete word *granted* in the sense of given, yielded, may take over the function of the colourless conjunction *although, even if*: "Granted she is unreliable, I still find her charming." An analogous shift is affecting the word *suppose*, which occasionally acts as substitute for the abstract conjunction *if*: "Suppose (or: supposing) you borrow some money, you'll be able to do this." The etymology of *suppose* points to spatial reference (Latin *sub+ponere, -positus*,

French *supposer* meaning to place something under something else), not hard to detect even today, but it now functions as an indicator of causal logical relationship. Sentence intonation shows that the two words in question, *directly* and *suppose*, do in fact introduce groups of words that are "dependent" (see the next section) on others, and at the same time they connect the two groups. Hence there is additional reason for calling both words conjunctions.[8]

An obvious conclusion of all this is that, if grammatical classes or parts of speech shift and overlap and sometimes evade classification within the limits of even one language, great care must be exercised in adapting its terminology (or any terminology, for that matter) for the description of another. The need for such caution may be demonstrated by a comparison of early pioneer descriptions of exotic languages with those made in recent times by trained linguists. In the New World as in Africa and Asia the first attempts to study the speech of native peoples were often made by Christian missionaries whose training was based on Latin. It is not strange, therefore, that they sought to describe the morphology, including the inflexions, of newly investigated, quite strange languages in terms of Latin grammar. In general, they expected and even tried to find grammatical categories to which they were accustomed. As a result, they sometimes created parts of speech which did not exist, and made inflexions of elements which could be more simply described in terms of word formation.

It is instructive, for instance, to compare two studies of Nahuatl, the language spoken by the Aztecs of Mexico and by their descendants today. In 1547, not very long after the conquest by the Spaniards, Friar Andres de Olmos wrote his *Arte para Aprender*

---

[8] Interestingly, a contracted form of *suppose*, pronounced *s'pose*, has been standardized in Melanesian Pidgin English as normal equivalent of the conjunction *if*. A sentence which may be roughly translated into conventional English spelling runs as follows: "S'pose you look-im man ee-kitch-im poison, you ee-can talk"; translated, it means "if you had seen the man who made black magic, you might talk." See Robert A. Hall, *Melanesian Pidgin English, Grammar, Texts, Vocabulary* (Baltimore, 1943), p. 45.

la Lengua Mexicana.[9] The effort was praiseworthy but the attitude was indicated by an initial statement: "In this language there are to be found all the parts of speech of Latin." As a result, the author identified as prepositions words which were really post-positions following their pronoun objects, and he presented full paradigms of verbs in what he called "moods" such as the subjunctive and infinitive and volitional, when these were no more than simple indicative tense forms accompanied by expressions meaning "if, it appears that," "one wishes," etc. In our times the structure of Nahuatl has been presented in vastly simplified form by a linguist[10] who recognized the role of free and bound forms in the language, and the way in which accompanying forms replace—but do not correspond to—the truly inflected conjugational bound forms of the Latin subjunctive and imperative. For instance, the stem *tla-pia* means to guard, and is inflected in present tense by prefixing bound forms of the personal pronouns: thus *ni-tla-pia* "I guard." All that distinguishes the so-called subjunctive and imperative moods is, according to Olmes himself, the use of *xi-* [ʃi] for the second person pronoun bound form in both singular and plural in place of *ti-/an-*, and the use of *ma* (corresponding to Polish *niech*) for a prefixed imperative sign-word; *yntla* for the subjunctive sign-word. Thus the whole paradigm can be enormously simplified.

Of course there are border-line cases. In Ewe, the African language already referred to, the plural of substantives is said to be formed by suffixing *-wo* to the singular. This sounds like an inflexion in the usual sense, comparable to *book-s* as the plural of English *book*, or *list-y* as the plural of Polish *list*. But on closer examination it turns out that the presumed suffix *-wo* is identical with the third personal pronoun *wo* meaning they. Moreover, it is not always added to the noun in question, but regularly to a post-positive adjective modifier. Thus while the plural of *ame* (meaning

---

⁹ Ed. from a manuscript in the Bibliothèque Nationale, Paris, by Rémi Siméon (Paris, 1875).

¹⁰ Richard Sanders Pittman, *A Grammar of Tetelcingo (Morales Nahuatl)*, Linguistic Society (Baltimore, 1954).

human beings) is *amewo*—which looks like an inflected plural—the plural of the expression meaning wild animals is one literally translatable as "animals-wild-they." It might be more accurate, therefore, to say that words classified for various reasons as nouns not only lack gender (as has been recognized) but also number. This latter is a grammatical category indicated for entire phrases as well as single words by the loose addition of a plural pronoun; the method is agglutination rather than suffixation.

In general it may be said that the simplest method of description is the best, provided only (and this is an important condition) that all relevant forms are taken into account. A description that fails to do so will be simplicistic (that is, misleading by very reason of its simplicity), as if for instance a description of plurality in English nouns were to confine itself to an account of the morpheme /s/ and its allomorphs, without considering the small group of forms such as *men, geese, mice,* where plurality is indicated by internal vowel change only.[11]

---

[11] In the special terminology of structural linguistics, units of grammatical feature indicating how sentence elements are arranged—groups of words, individual words, and morphemes—are called taxemes. They are said to include four types: (1) selection, (2) order, (3) modulation and (4) phonetic modification. By selection is meant categorization or classification: a constituent form belongs to a class which may or may not take another form following it (for instance, the English noun *count* has a feminine form *count-ess,* but most nouns are excluded from this modification). The feature of order simply refers to the position of a given element in relation to others, whether preceding or following. Modulation refers to the incidence of stress (for instance, the *-ess* suffix is always unstressed). Phonetic modification appears when two grammatically related forms are distinguished by variation in their sounds: before the suffix *-ess, duke* is changed to *duch-ess.* A taxeme, taken by itself, may have no meaning; when one or more taken together do have meaning the combination is called a tagmeme (for instance, *duch + ess*).
   Thus far Leonard Bloomfield, *Language* (New York, 1933), pp. 166-68. The list of tagmemes, it should be noticed, takes into account only grammatical traits of sequential relationship. There are however correspondences which occur regardless of order: e.g. the correspondence of endings to be found in both *dominām bonām* and *bonam dominam.*—Again, the appearance of one vowel rather than another in strong verbs is surely a grammatical feature, but it has nothing to do with linear sequence. Here perhaps it would

4. SYNTAX, OR THE RELATION OF SENTENCE ELEMENTS

Single words are often capable of conveying much grammatical information by themselves; in inflected languages especially, they may indicate such categories as singularity versus duality and/or plurality, adherence to classes sometimes known as genders, modifications indicating case, and so on. When single words appear in configurations—that is to say together with other words grouped in sentences (as previously defined)—they are said to be in syntactic relationship. *Syntax* is a Greek word meaning arrangement together. It implies, obviously, a minimum of two elements. Syntax, then, is devoted primarily to the study of groups of words in utterances rather than single words and their modifications.

This is but a rough-and-ready definition, to be sure. Not all authorities agree in their delimitation of syntax as opposed to inflexional morphology. Leonard Bloomfield has stated[12] that "Syntactic constructions, then, are constructions in which none of the immediate constituents is a bound form." (For an explanation of bound forms, see ch. 3, sec. 1.) Of course it is necessary to define what a construction is, in the first place. The dividing up of sentences into IC's is not always an easy matter. The first step may be obvious enough, as when the English sentence "This is the pen with which I write" is broken down into a subject of discourse *this* and a predication consisting of the rest of the utterance. The latter in turn can be broken down into a verb-form *is* followed by a predicative capable of further subdivision into smaller elements, ending in this case in single words. But the boundaries are not always clear, as can be seen by comparing the two following English sentences:

(1) This is what | I write with |
(2) | I write with my pen |

---

be better to speak of a taxeme of selection, in the sense that the speaker "chooses" among various forms at his disposal, all of which would be equally permissible within the framework of preceding and following morphemes. In that case, Bloomfield's first taxeme might be renamed the taxeme of classification. It would seem that the terminology of taxemics requires further study.

12 Bloomfield, *op. cit.*, p. 184.

The vertical lines mark off major IC's.[13] In the first example *with* is tied up with *write*, and looks backward, as it were; in the second it looks forward. There is no bound form here. The two words *write* and *with* are both free, yet whether they make up a syntactic construction when taken together has to be further determined.

It is an important task in describing any language to indicate how the major and minor elements of sentences are related to one another. The following modes or relationship are the ones most frequently to be found, whether singly or in combination.

Order is the simplest, least complicated method to be described. If it is known that of two nouns placed in sequence, the first will always modify or limit the meaning of the second, then it is easy to interpret the syntactic construction "chief-house" to mean "house of the chief." Conversely, if it is known that the second will always modify the first, then it is easy to interpret "house-chief" in the same way. Chinese, in its many forms and dialects, offers the classical example of order as the basis of syntax. English relies greatly on the same method, though to a less degree. It is only order that indicates which part of the sentence refers to the subject of the verb and which to its object in a statement like "The boy saw the farmer." Here a change of order "The farmer saw the boy" involves a change of meaning. (Not so, of course, in more inflected languages like German and Polish, where a change of order is possible without change of meaning. It is syntactically indifferent whether one says "Der Knabe sah den Bauer" or "Den Bauer sah der Knabe"; "Chłopak widział rolnika" or "Rolnika widział chłopak.") Insofar as inflexion exists, even to a limited extent, it will encroach upon the domain of order as a determinant of syntax. Even to this day, English "Him do I accuse" is the same in meaning, hence is equivalent to, "I do accuse him." To be sure, there is here a difference in emphasis, which is a matter of style (see below), but the inflexional contrast of the pronoun *he: him*

---

[13] One might compare Polish *On stał obok* with *Pałac stał obok kościoła*. Here as in the English examples, intonation may give a clue to the boundaries, but not always.

permits the variation in word order without sacrifice of syntactic clarity.

Congruence or agreement is another well-known method of grouping individual words or expressions together syntactically. Similarity or identity of inflexional endings is one, but only one, sign of congruence among forms. In Latin, the expression *regīna magna et bona* is tied together by obvious means (compare Polish *królowa wielka i dobra*), namely by repetition of the ending -*a*. Correlations of a less obvious sort are also possible, as when it is found that certain recognizable forms are regularly associated with others even though the endings are not identical, as Latin *poēta, agrīcola, nauta* are tied together with modifiers like *magnus* and *bonus* (not *magna* and *bona* as might be expected; compare Polish *poeta wielki,* not *wielka*). Whether or not the alignment is obvious, it can be established by tests of substitution. It is thus that covert or concealed relationships become overt. In English there are very few nouns that can be classified according to the category of gender (masculine, feminine or neuter) by purely morphological evidence. But congruence of third person pronouns with nouns they replace gives the required key: "I spoke to his wife and she said..." (not *he* said...). In some languages the congruence is made very obvious; in others, less so.

Government or control of one linguistic form by another is still another method indicating syntactic relationship. As the term implies, two forms are related in discourse in such a way that one obliges the appearance of another type of form preceding or following it, but without a mutual sharing of grammatical characteristics. Herein lies the important distinction between congruence and government. An adjective may share in the categories of gender and number with the noun it accompanies, as may verbal forms with their subjects (e.g. Latin *dominus amātus est,* Polish *pan miał*): in this situation there is congruence. But a verb or a preposition may call for a given form (case) of its object, regardless of its own form. Latin *credere* and Polish *ufać,* both meaning to believe, are both followed by nouns or pronouns in what is traditionally known as the dative case, regardless of the tense, person or number of the verbs. In the same way, prepositions or postpositions, themselves uninflected, may call for a given inflectional form (case) of a noun or pronoun associated with them: Latin *cum dominō* or *cum dominā* or *mē-cum* (compare Polish *z panem, z panią, ze mną*). Here the prepositions are themselves unchanging, hence not subject to inflection, but the accompanying substantives assume necessary modifications conditioned by them. (Among such modifications may be vowel quantity.)

In some languages, groups of words functioning as longer or shorter constituents may perform the function of single parts of speech. In English, one may say "The top man" or "The man on top" or "The man holding the top position" or "The man who is on top." The similarity in meaning and function of the word-groups containing *top* leads to the conclusion that all of them are modifiers of *man*. In this way we come to the conclusion that some sentence elements may be subordinated to others or, as is commonly said, be dependent on them. Some specialists use the expression endocentric construction for a phrase belonging to the same form class as one of its elements, as in the phrase just cited. An exocentric construction would then be one belonging to a form-class other than any of its constituents: e.g. the sentence "He came," which performs a function of complete predication, differing from the function of any of its parts.

Just as it is important to describe word classes ("parts of speech") and their modifications in terms of each language, without imposing categories from without, so it is important to describe syntactic relations in the same way. It has been mentioned (above, sec. 3) that in the Mende language of West Africa, the personal pronouns are inflected by alternation of vowels and by changes in tone—to indicate changes of tense and, also, as it happens, to indicate whether the predicated action is positive or negative. Prefixed and suffixed particles loosely attached to the verbs also indicate tenses in both the positive and negative conjugations. To an extent, therefore, there is congruence or agreement between the pronoun forms and the verbal particles. But the latter are not in any way modified according to the person and number of the pronoun subject. There is no trace of congruence in this respect. The pronominal paradigm having been once established, the description of verbs in relation to it can be greatly simplified. It is not necessary to write out for the present perfect tense of pe_3 (meaning to do)[14] the following scheme:

Singular	ngi_4	pe_3	nga_3	Plural	mu_4	pe_3	nga_3
	bi_4	pe_3	nga_3		wu_4	pe_3	nga_3
	i_2	pe_3	nga_3		ti_4	pe_3	nga_3

It is enough to state: the present perfect tense is formed by suffixing-nga_3 to the verbal root; with it are associated the positive or negative pronouns of the past and perfect inflexion used as subjects.[15] This formulation is simpler, and just as accurate. Syntactic description is here obviously closely related to inflexional.

From the point of view of a child learning to speak his native tongue at the usual tender age, there is no such thing as a difficult linguistic structure. From the point of view of adult learners, however, it will appear that there is a wide range between the simpler and more complicated types. Mere juxtaposition of words without inflexion, without requirements of congruence or government, may be taken as representing a simple type of syntax—though it may be rendered very complex by patterns of intonation with syntactic implications. At the other extreme there are languages in which syntactic correlations are overtly expressed by complicated correlations throughout an entire sentence. Among these are languages of the Bantu family in Africa. In all of these the words (nouns) which may stand in the head position of a complete utterance are found to belong to clearly defined classes, each

---

[14] Subscript numbers refer to tones.

[15] In her useful and clear description, *A Grammar of the Mende Language* (Philadelphia, 1935), Ethel G. Aginsky does not avail herself of this simplified method of presenting the relationship between verb form and subject. For each tense she repeats the paradigm of positive and negative pronoun forms, already established, together with the unchanging verbal form that goes with it. She thus tries without warrant to make the verbal conjugation appear to possess person and number, which it does not.

of them identifiable by a prefix subject to regular modifications throughout the sentence, according to the word it is attached to, but always pointing back to the one in head position. Here is an example from the Temne language, where the class-marker of the first word is a long *o*, written *ō*:

ō. bai	ō. we	ō. bi	ō. tem	ō. fi
the-chief	the-this	the-black	the-wise	he-died

meaning "This wise black chief died." Or this from the Dyōla language:

fu. nuk	fu. bak	a. fu	du	fu. ruk	f'an	fu. dak
the-stick	the-long	this	and	it-thick	it-which	it-is-good

i. nōme fω[16]
I buy   it

meaning "This long and thick stick which seems all right, I buy it." The choice of the first word is the speaker's, of course. But once he has chosen it, he is committed to a pattern of echoing references all pointing back to the initial term. He is bound, in other words, to a complex system of internal congruence.

5. Some Stylistic Implications of Linguistic Structure

The possibility of various means of linguistic expression within a single accepted code or *langue* leads to the problem of style. About this little can be said here. Individual style in language implies a choice. If a writer or speaker is compelled to use recognized formulas, as for instance in traditional religious ritual, in military dispatches, scientific reports or the like, he will have no chance to develop a personal style. The one he follows was already set down for him by others, fixed by social institutions on the basis of long collective experiences. Once there may have been choice of a sort, but it ended in prescription. On the other hand a writer or speaker may develop a distinctive style of his own, likewise based on the choice available to him within the materials and the organizational patterns of his language.

---

[16] The Greek character ω stands for a diphthong approximating English [ou].

All aspects of a language, its range of phonemes (including those of pitch and accent), its system of morphemes and their combinations, its syntactic structure, vocabulary and word order— all of them represent a complex interrelation of freedom and restrictions. A language like the Hawaiian of the Polynesian group, which is characterized by a predominance of open syllables, a paucity of consonants and high frequency in the use of vowels, is by nature equipped to create aesthetic effects (popularly labelled as "liquid, lyrical," etc.) contrasting with those of a language which frequently employs heavy consonant clusters, closed syllables and strong dynamic stress. The incidence of a fixed stress will have definite consequences for the versification of poetry. In Polish the universal requirement of penultimate accentuation of polysyllables means the exclusion of iambic lines with masculine endings. Highly developed inflexions multiply the possibilities for rhyme effects as in expressions like Latin *illārum bonārum fēminārum* (the equivalent of "those good women"). Besides, the inflexions—as we have seen—permit freedom of word order, so that the placement of sentence elements becomes a matter of rhetorical effect for emphasis, suspense, delay and the like. Uninflected or only slightly inflected languages may lack resources of this kind, but on the other hand they more readily achieve emphasis by conciseness and economy of expression. Again, the current vocabulary may be homogenous (as in modern Icelandic) or diversified by many loan words (as in modern English). This too has implications for stylistic effect.

Granted these preconditions implicit in linguistic systems themselves, there still remain wide areas of choice in each. At the very least it is useful to distinguish what has been called casual from noncasual use of a language. The former is on the whole spontaneous and unreflecting; the writer or speaker does not consciously plan his style. The latter is on the other hand deliberately planned, as in formal oratory, in advertizing, in poetry and other forms of literary expression. This division is, however, a very general one. Depending on social conditions, especially class stratification, there may be various levels of style within the type of discourse known as casual. There can be informal educated speech, very colloquial speech, and finally a kind of speech not considered acceptable among persons of education and social status, even when they are being most informal. The relationship of these types of casual discourse among themselves calls for a recognition of factors of environment which belong partly to the field of sociology. The availability of education, or the lack of it, is one such factor.

For the study of non-casual style there is a long European tradition extending back to classical times. The Greeks became consciously aware of stylistic values implicit in their language and investigated them especially in relation to the practice of oratory. For effective speaking in public debates it was important to know what patterns of sound would be pleasing at the ends of sentences; what arrangements of word order and syntactic constructions would be effective by contributing to the listeners' suspense and his interest and lucid understanding; what figures of speech would appropriately embellish the discourse in various contexts. Greek handbooks of rhetoric, dealing with these matters, were adapted by the Romans. They were transmitted into the Middle Ages and became the foundation of teaching the subject in the Renaissance and in modern times.

This classical tradition (directly from the Greeks in much of Eastern Europe, through the Romans generally in Western Europe) has very largely shaped our stylistics (that is, our study of style) down to the present. We have learned from it how to exploit the resources of vernacular languages for artistic purposes. In each instance there has resulted what may be called a "literary" type of speech and writing within the framework of the national language. Common to it are the accepted usages and the recognized devices of effective discourse known to all who engage in non-casual writing or speaking.

But each writer or speaker also shows his originality to a greater or less degree in availing himself of the general literary conventions and patterns already established. Innovation in the handling of language is also important.

Here we are confronted with a special sort of problem. The individual's experimental use of language for artistic expression may go so far as to reduce its power of communication very seriously, so far as the average reader or listener is concerned. It is true that certain schools of writers have in the past cultivated very elaborate styles designed for special audiences: for instance, the Old Icelandic skaldic poets, the Provençal troubadours, the composers of 17th century *concetti* (poetic conceits, as they are called in English) in the school of Marini. But in our time some writers of prose as well as verse have had recourse to many devices baffling linguistic arrangement, sometimes inexplicable except by the individual author. In this respect they differ from practitioners of elaborate styles in the past, who at least belonged to definable schools with traditional techniques well recognized.

Modern formalists have claimed that a writer's individual style represents a "violence" done to the language in which he expresses himself. It has been assumed that the literary artist must necessarily be "different" in the use of his medium—even to the point of incomprehensibility, if he so desires. This thesis raises two important questions. The first one is: To what extent can a literary artist abandon the normal channels of linguistic communication without losing contact with the public? The second is: Does the artist really wish to establish contact with his public?

The second question does not fall within the province of linguists. The first, however, has some relevance to that discipline. If a literary artist, for all his originality and his experimental use of language, still wishes to remain in contact with his audience, then the linguist may help in keeping the channel of communication open. The linguist may elucidate the technique employed by the artist. And it may turn out that the "violence" was after all not so great as was at first supposed.

The possibility of fruitful collaboration between linguists and interpreters of literature has been increasingly recognized in the past few years. Conferences have been devoted to the discussion of stylistic problems, in which specialists in both fields participated. A very stimulating conference, organized on an international scale,

was held in Warsaw (1960), devoted to the problem of poetics:
that is, one specific domain of literary style in general. The contributions by professional linguists demonstrated how helpful their
work could be, not only for the elucidation of difficult literary
texts, but for a deepening of the aesthetic pleasure to be derived
from them.[17]

---

[17] The papers given at this conference have been published in a volume of
893 pages under the title *Poetics* (Warsaw, Państwowe Wydawnictwo Nau-
kowe, 1961). The five languages of the conference are represented in the
contributions: English, French, German, Polish, Russian.

CHAPTER 7

CONTEMPORARY APPROACHES TO THE PROBLEMS OF LANGUAGE

1. LANGUAGE AND THE THEORY OF PROBABILITY

When someone speaks, he emits a series of sounds which can be identified, as we have been seen, as phonemes constituting morphemes, and the morphemes are in turn organized in some way to indicate their mutual relationships: whether by simple juxtaposition or by inflexional correspondences, or by patterns of repeated correlation of a general sort, it does not matter. In any event, the series of sounds emitted between one major pause (or major juncture, as it may be called) and another can be designated as an utterance, as previously explained.

An utterance of this sort is acoustically (as we have seen) a continuum. The hesitations of a stammerer, which have to be taken into account in some types of analysis, do not affect this statement, for it is easy to make bridges across the gaps in his discourse originating in non-linguistic causes. But from the point of view of the listener the continuum is perceived discretely: i.e., as a series of separate units in sequence.

A linguistic sequence of this sort shows characteristics that can be described in terms of statistical probability. When an utterance begins with a specific morpheme of the class M_1, one may ask: What are the probabilities that it will be followed by a morpheme of the class M_2?—and so on. The question resembles that of a card player holding a set of cards in his hands and asking himself: What are my chances of winning the game? Or the question of a human being of any age asking himself: What are my chances of surviving until the end of this year? The serious study of such problems began historically with an inquiry into the phenomena of gambling. People were curious to know about their likelihood of making a certain throw of the dice, or of obtaining a desired combination of cards. Later they became interested in their likelihood of survival at a given age, and on the basis of this interest there were collected the vast data which enable life insurance companies to function so effectively. Such companies can tell you that, on the basis of past knowledge and experience, there is a likelihood amounting almost to certainty that out of so-and-so many citizens of a certain group, so-and-so many will die before the end of the year. Of course, this does not mean that any specific Citizen X is doomed to die any more than Citizen Y, but the mortal chances of both are subject to mathematical calculation, granted normal conditions. (It must be admitted that extraordinary events such as visitations of plague on a wide scale several times experienced in the Middle Ages or atomic explosions as practised in our own times, introduce a new factor not easily dealt with.)

Statistical studies in any field of human behaviour are based on the frequency of the appearance of certain phenomena in relation to other phenomena. In English, it is found that the word "the" is highly likely to be followed by other words of a certain definable group, but not by words of other groups. Thus speakers of English will accept an utterance beginning "The man...," "The man-power," "The mandrake...," "The mandate..." and so on, but will not accept an utterance beginning "The thinks..." or even "The mankind..." From such observations it is possible to make deductions concerning the kinds of words or individual morphemes which may follow an initial *the*: and even more than that, it is possible to estimate the relative probability that the word following *the* will itself be followed by one morpheme sequence rather than any other of those available in the English language. To do this it would of course be necessary to tabulate examples taken from extremely abundant materials: millions of words in connected discourse. However, this can be done. It would then appear that the simplex form *man* has the highest probability rating of all, as might be expected. The compound noun *man-power* would be likely to come next. The word *mandate* might stand at least as high; but this a tricky example. Historically the element *man-* has nothing to do with the English homonymous morpheme, being derived ultimately from Latin *manus* meaning a hand; a mandate was a contract in the sense of a hand-giving. True enough, this fact has little meaning from the synchronic point of view, and it may well be that many speakers of English today, lacking a classical education, would identify this *man-* with the word *man*, just as many identify the first element in *sextette* (meaning six) with the homonymous morpheme *sex*. The frequency of *man-* versus *man* would however have to be established by systematic investigation. The same problems would arise in connexion with the less familiar words *mandrake* and *mandragora*, having low frequencies.

Finally, the sequence *the + mankind* would have a probability tantamount to zero, if it were not for the inherent possibility that some stylistic innovator—say a poet—might initiate this sequence as a result of artistic experimentation on the language. He may write a line: "The mankind unkind ever-linked waves of our being," thus trying by word-play to drive home the point that human beings are both linked and yet separated in the series of their generations. They are, he says, united yet hostile. If this phrase should catch on in current speech and be many times quoted, the probability of the sequence *the + mankind* would of course rise considerably. At this point we must reckon with a combination of factors: sociological (why was the historical situation of the English-speaking world favourable to the acceptance of such a sentiment?), aesthetic (why are the echoed sounds and rhythms pleasing to the ear?) and linguistic (why and how does the English language place such resources at the disposal of the poet?). The interplay of such factors has not yet been adequately investigated for non-casual discourse (see ch. 6, sec. 5).

The probabilities for the appearance of specific words in non-poetic discourse has been investigated on a comparative basis for English, French, German and Spanish by Helen Eaton. True enough, she relied on earlier studies based on written, not oral materials. True enough, her results should now be verified in the light of our wider knowledge of spoken discourse. Nevertheless, her findings may still be valuable for someone writing an elementary textbook for the teaching of one of the languages mentioned.

He will want to know what are the words having the highest frequency of usage, so that he may concentrate on them. Besides, results such as these may open up a field for later investigations into the psychological significance of vocabulary distribution. It may be significant of something not purely linguistic that the Spanish word *santo* stands among the first 500 of the first thousand when ranked for frequency; the French *saint* and German *heilig* appear in the second 500, and English *holy* is classified lower, in the second thousand. French *idée* and Spanish *idea* are slightly higher than German *Begriff*, which appears in the second half of the first thousand, while English *idea* is like *holy* relegated to the second thousand. On the other hand English *fair* in the sense of just enjoys a high position among the top 500 words on the English list, as do also French *droit* and *juste*; Spanish *justo* is only a bit lower, while German *gerecht* and *ehrlich* are relegated to the second thousand. It would be premature to deduce from this that speakers of English are more concerned with matters of fair play than with abstract ideas (*Begriffe*), and speakers of German vice versa. Still, it would seem that some sort of connexion could well be established between cultural phenomena and vocabulary frequency, especially on a comparative basis.[1]

The probability of the appearance of one phoneme after another can also be investigated. This is not the same as the probability of one written letter following another, especially in languages with

---

[1] See Helen Eaton, *Semantic Frequency List for English, French, German, and Spanish* (New York, 1940); reprinted as *Word Frequency Dictionary* (New York: Dover Publications, 1961). The author presents material derived from previous studies, here systematically arranged. For the German she has relied on F. W. Kaeding, *Häufigkeitswörterbuch der deutschen Sprache* (Berlin, 1898). This work, though no doubt valuable at its time, was already long out of date when Miss Easton's study was undertaken. The studies on French, English and Spanish were done in the late 1920's and early 1930's. It would be interesting to verify the extent to which political events in the 1940's and 1950's may have shifted the frequency ratings of certain words, e.g. *aggression* (low on the English list, high as *Angriff* on the German: but *non-aggression* must have represented a frequent variant in all languages on the eve of World War II).

archaic orthography like English and French. Still, both of these are subject to investigations. An early example of the application of probability theory to English spelling will be found in a short story by Edgar Allan Poe called "The Gold Bug." A message concerning hidden treasure, written by Captain Kidd, the famous pirate, has been encoded, as we should now say, in symbols consisting of numbers and conventional signs such as ☿,) ' and †. The discoverer of the message begins with a knowledge that *e* is the letter most frequently used in English spelling; he knows the descending rank of the others as well. He also knows that *e* is often doubled in English spelling, and that the word *the* is the one most frequently used. This knowledge leads him to identify the symbols for other letters, as he proceeds from decipherment of *the* to *tree* to *degree* and so on to final decipherment of the entire message. To this day the method of decipherment employed by Poe is interesting, although our techniques have gone far beyond anything he could have imagined.

2. LANGUAGE AND COMMUNICATION THEORY

Poe's story, simple as it is, suggests other problems of linguistic communication, whether spoken or written, in which frequency and probability play a role.

Some three decades ago, G. K. Zipf undertook to investigate what relation, if any, exists between the length of words and their frequency of occurrence in sample languages chosen for investigation. He came to the conclusion that the length of a word tends to decrease as its relative frequency of use increases. Thus the neologism of the first years of this century, *automobile*, yielded place to *auto* or *car* in English (compare Polish *wóz*); *gasoline* to *gas*, etc. The shortness or length of a word is not the cause of its greater or less frequency, but on the contrary the frequency is the cause of the relative shortness. This general trend was related by Zipf to an underlying "law" of the economy of effort in speaking. He deduced a general formula, $ab^2 = k$, in which *a* stands for the number of words having a given frequency of occurrence (e.g., how many words are used as frequently as English *this* or Polish *to* ?) and *b* stands for the number of their occurrences (for instance, as estimated on a semantic frequency list). The latter *k* simply means that the result is a constant. In other words, there is a constant, predictable relationship between length and frequency.

Zipf attempted to discover in the same way the predictable relationships between efforts in enunciation ("phonetic difficulty") and frequency of occurrence of individual phonemes, besides other linguistic correlations. His methods and his results have been criticized, but his work offered a valuable stimulus leading to further studies, and the formula just mentioned has come to be known as "Zipf's Law," often quoted if also sometimes questioned.

Somewhat later, G. U. Yule employed statistical investigations as a test for the determination of the authorship of a disputed literary work. Yule made frequent reference to Zipf's studies. The impetus for his inquiry was the question whether the *Imitatio Christi*, written in Latin in the 15th century, was the work of Jean Gerson or Thomas à Kempis, and this led to a statistical analysis of the vocabulary frequencies in the known works of both authors. More recently, G. Herdan has developed the same technique and likewise applied it (among other things) to a question of disputed authorship. In this case the question was whether a recently discovered scientific text in English of the late 14th century, *The Equatorie of the Planetis*, could be attributed to the poet Geoffrey Chaucer, who is known with certainty to be the author of an analogous work called *The Book of the Astrolabe*. Herdan's conclusion, based on a statistical analysis of the two texts, was positive.

Engineers have understandably been interested in the statistical investigation of language—especially engineers concerned with the efficient transmission of information by such means as telegraphy, telephones, navy signalling, radio and so on. All of these means are substitutions for an elementary situation in which one person talks to another directly. In all of them there is a series of signals emitted by a sender, a channel of communication, and a receiver of the signals. But there must also exist a code or general system of interpreting the signals. The Morse code enables us to translate dots and dashes into the letters of a written language. Similarly, the code of correspondences between arbitrary signs and letters, once it was understood, enabled the hero of Poe's tale to interpret a secret message as a normal one. Finally, every spoken language represents a code (de Saussure's *langue*) or general scheme in terms of which every individual message or utterance may be understood (deciphered) by the receiver.

All this is fairly obvious. But there are problems connected with the efficiency of the code and the efficiency of the channel of transmission. The code may offer contrasts on the order of word units which are nearly always clear (as in Polish) or it may contain numerous ambiguities as does English, with its multiple homonyms such as *pain*: *pane*, *sea*: *see*, *pail*: *pale*, *sole*: *soul*, and many others. Individual signals (letters, dot-and-dash combinations, phonemes) may be confusingly alike. Besides, other factors may disturb the channel of transmission. In a specific act of communication there may be external influences tending to a diminution of understanding. When two people talk in a crowded room full of other people talking, or when a telephone conversation is hampered by a bad connexion, there is said to be noise. In other words, noise is anything which hampers communication. Engineers in the field of communication must of course be concerned with the purely physical factors of noise such as poor wire connexions, but they are also interested in factors of a linguistic nature. They want to know what linguistic contrasts may be the clearest and hence least subject to interference by noise of any sort, and what contrasts may be less clear and therefore more subject to interference.

An utterance, no matter how transmitted, is often referred to as a Markoff chain, namely a series or process in which the probabilities depend on the previous events. The name is taken from the Russian scholar A. A. Markoff (Markov) who made a pioneer study of a problem concerning the distribution of vowels and consonants in a literary text, and showed that the transitional probabilities between the letters were not random but dependent on preceding items in the chain.[2] This conclusion may seem fairly obvious, but it is important when related to the question: How much information is transmitted by each unit in the series; and: How efficient is the channel of transmission?

Communications engineers interested in language as a code have worked out a method of calculating mathematically the amount of information conveyed by any unit in a Markoff chain. Briefly speaking, it depends on the number of yes-and-no questions required to identify the unit concerned. (Those who have played the game of twenty questions are familiar with the technique.) The information obtained by the answer to one such question is called a binit or a bit, derived from the expression "binary digit." Pursuing this method of successive subdivisions by means of simple binary choices, it will be found that the total number of questions x required to identify N number of objects can be expressed in terms of the logarithm having a base 2 (not 10, as in the logarithmic tables we normally use). The formula is: $x = \log_2 N$. The situation may be clarified by a table in which 8 objects, lettered A to H, are grouped according to successive subdivisions indicated by positive $(+)$ or negative $(-)$ answers to questions of classification:[3]

	A	B	C	D	E	F	G	H
Question 1	−	−	−	−	+	+	+	+
Question 2	−	−	+	+	−	−	+	+
Question 3	−	+	−	+	−	+	−	+

The essential groupings here resulted from three fundamental questions, and 3 is the power to which 2 must be raised in order to obtain the number 8. In other words, as far as information goes,

---

[2] The literary text analyzed was Pushkin's *Eugene Onegin*; the units, it will be noticed, were letters of the Russian alphabet, not phonemes of the spoken language. The study was published in French in the *Bulletin* of the Imperial Academy of Sciences, VII (St. Petersburg, 1913).

[3] This figure is taken, slightly modified, from C. Colin Cherry, Morris Halle and Roman Jakobson, "Toward the Logical Description of Languages in heir Phonemic Aspect," *Language*, XXIX (1953), 34–46, Fig. I.

the 8 objects have a log_2 of 3. To take a concrete example, we may wish to classify a series of phonemes and go about it by asking such questions as: nasal or non-nasal? voiced or unvoiced? spirant or stop? and so on. The number of questions required is obviously related to the amount of information we obtain concerning the precise nature of the phoneme.

Of course, the situation is not always so ideally clear as in the scheme just presented. For instance, the number of items to be classified is often not a power of 2. Or again, the answer to the yes-or-no question may be an unequal subdivision or a response meaning indifferent. (Such answers may be represented schematically by the sign for zero ø, or by $\pm$). For one classification of phonemes in English, namely the consonants, the question of nasality is pertinent, but not for the vowels. On the other hand nasality is pertinent in Polish and French for both vowels and consonants. This is simply another way of stating the principle of minimal pairs or essential contrasts within linguistic systems.

When such situations arise in the tabulation of information, the results of the basic formula $x = log_2 N$ must inevitably be fractions. At first glance this must seem silly. How can one have a fraction of a piece of information? But the question can be resolved by appealing once more to the theory of probability based on statistics. A gambler will tell you that he has a five to two chance of winning in a game of chance (let us say, in a horse-race). He may be right or wrong, but his guess is expressed as a fraction. So also with information. Here too the load of information may be expressed in fractions.

And now we come to a very important problem. Suppose that the load of information in a given signal is practically nil. In English spelling, the letter q is automatically followed by the letter u (as in *quit, quiet*, etc.); only very rarely followed by other letters—as in transcriptions from Arabic, where q stands for voiceless velar consonant not represented in English. In such ion practically no information is conveyed by the letter answer to the question Yes or No will be automatic: re. Here the index of information is therefore, one might say, zero. But in the realm of practical affairs such a sequence may be useful.

Suppose for instance you receive a telegram in English distorted to read QBESTION BNANSWERED. You know that the predicability of -*u* following *q*- in English is almost 100%. Hence you have no trouble in substituting *u* for *b* in the message received. In diminishing degrees the predicability of other sequences can also be established. These are what are called transitional probabilities. When the transitional probability is in effect one (or 100%) as in the likelihood of an English *u* following the letter *q*, one might say that the second letter is redundant. Similarly there are some phonetic traits of phonemes which may be called redundant, since they are not strictly essential for their identification. But redundancy may be valuable. When noise interferes (as in a garbled telegram or a bad telephone connexion or a disturbed conversation) it is good to have extra binits of information at our disposal. And these may be represented in terms of transitional probabilities: for instance, if we are in doubt whether a given English word is *thinks* or the slang word *finks* (both begun with voiceless spirants distinguished by only one feature equivalent to one binit of information) we are aided by the context and its probabilities. If the preceding word is *he*, the probability is close to one (100%) that the word should be *thinks*; if it is *the*—it should be *finks* (a noun meaning a special kind of gangster).

The term entropy, borrowed from physics where it means a state of disorder and its measurement, has been adopted by some writers on the theory of communication. They would have it that information is negative entropy or the opposite of disorder. But others have warned against the use of this term as a misleading analogy. In physics, entropy refers to a thermodynamic system. But a language code is not such a system, since it is clear that any number of listeners may receive an identical message (for instance by radio or television) on the basis of the same expenditure of time and energy. Hence informational entropy, whether positive or negative, here differs from thermodynamics, which is subjected to purely physical laws of efficiency.

One fact emerges from all discussions of language in relation to the theory of communication. Redundancy may represent a loss in communication if one is speaking in terms of an ideally efficient system. But in terms of a system subject to noise, as in human speech, redundancy helps to ensure effective transmission.

The measurement of linguistic phenomena by binits of information suggests at once the use of computers and similar mechanical aids widely used in other fields such as book-keeping. It suggests in fact techniques leading to machine translation. Metaphorically, it is possible to think of the human brain, when receiving linguistic stimuli, as a machine receiving "instructions." (This last word, commonly employed in describing mechanical functioning, is itself a metaphor in such a context.) Conversely, it is possible to think of a machine as a model of the human brain. Up to a certain point the analogy holds. But Colin Cherry, one of the pioneers in the investigation of human communication from an engineer's point of view, has himself warned against the dangers of such an analogy. When we speak of instruction, memory and decisions in relation to a machine we are employing a misleading metaphor. Human memory has properties far more complex than those characterizing a machine's static accumulation and storage of data. Science recognizes a fundamental distinction between organic and inorganic receivers of stimuli or "instructions." The latter type of receivers may be enormously complicated and highly efficient, thanks to more and more numerous technical devices employed. Yet they will always remain essentially different from organic receptors, just as purely physical or chemical phenomena are essentially different from biological. One might say that we are dealing with qualitative, not merely quantitative differences, and this should of course be kept in mind.

At the same time there is no reason to fear or reject the help of machines, as do some conservative linguists. Mechanical aids are surely welcome in matters of human communication, just as they have been for a long time in matters of human transportation. At all times in the history of technology, the question has arisen: will this invention serve human progress and tend to its survival, or will it hasten its destruction? The replacement of human translators by machines—even to a limited extent—raises the same question as the discovery of fire in ancient times, and the release of atomic energy in our own. In all such situations there were some factors of danger involved. We can only hope and struggle (and this is not a question of linguistics but of social history) so that mechanical aids will contribute to more efficient communication and mutual understanding among human beings, and not to the frustration of their communication or to the increase of misunderstandings.

3. Some Contemporary Analyses of Language

Communication theory, as applied to language, concentrates on the kind of situation in which an individual speaker addresses himself to a listener and evokes a reply from him. Some linguists of the school commonly called structuralist have associated their descriptions of such a situation with psychological behaviourism based on philosophical mechanism and solipsism. Their critics regard these descriptions as misleading because over-simple. A corrective has been sought by taking into account a wider area of social behaviour than the isolated person-to-person situation of linguistic communication. (See ch. 4, sec. 1.)

Social behaviourism is the term which has been applied to this general approach. A chief exponent is Kenneth Pike, who has made an ambitious effort[4] to correlate language phenomena with more general patterns of human behaviour. His terminology is based on a distinction between what he calls "etic" and "emic" descriptions. The two neologisms are derived from the familiar suffixes in the words *phonetic* and *phonemic*. Just as a phonetic transcription must be complete and detailed enough to record all acoustic nuances of pronunciation, regardless of the language concerned, so an "etic" description of social behaviour will have

---

[4] K. Pike, *Language in Relation to a Unified Theory of the Structure of Human Behaviour*, 3 vols., photo-offset (Glendale, California: Summer Institute of Linguistics, 1954–60).

to be comparative and intercultural (for instance, an analysis of burial ceremonies in a wide range of cultures). On the other hand, an "emic" description will be given in terms of one culture alone. Pike begins by defining a large sociological unit known as the behavioureme, that is to say a unified sequence of human actions—not limited to speech—controlled by known procedures in a set sequence: for instance, a church service, a football game, even a family breakfast. Here individual actions fall into place according to patterns. Within the behavioureme Pike finds "emic" motifs. An uttereme (contracted from utterance-eme) is a verbal behavioureme; an acteme is a minimal (that is, indivisible) uttereme. If it is verbal, it is a phoneme, relevant to one language alone; if it is non-verbal, it is a kineme or minimal motion (gesture). Thus Pike descends from major complexes of behaviour to minor and minimal. The effort at an integration of linguistic and non-linguistic phenomena of behaviour is praiseworthy as well as ambitious. However, the very artificial terminology may discourage others from following in his path. Besides, Pike's own classifications may sometimes be questioned. He speaks thus of the first gesture involved in buttering a piece of toast at breakfast, namely the grasping of the knife. This, he says, "is the first acteme (kineme) in a sequence of actemes which makes up the manifestation mode of that emic motif" (II, 1; 8:21). But is it really "emic" (to use Pike's term)? Surely the grasping of a knife, even to butter toast, is not confined to a single culture? Is it not then rather "etic" (again to use Pike's term)?

The merit of Pike's work is that he attempted to relate linguistics to a "Matrix of Social Behavior," as he called it. Of course he accepts the matrix as a fixed datum, and he does not look for the dynamics which may lead to change. But he did call attention to the wider implications of social environment in speech situations, thus diverging from Bloomfield.

Glossematics is the name given to a special type of descriptive analysis of language. The term comes from the originator of the system, the Danish scholar Louis Hjemslev, who has worked out for his purpose an elaborate and highly special terminology resembling that of formal logic. (His debt to R. Carnap's logical positivism is freely acknowledged.) The approach to language as a phenomenon to be analyzed is deductive and empirical. Theory itself is said (in the author's meaning) to be independent of experience. The purpose is to reveal what Hjemslev calls the "immanent" structure of a given language, quite apart from conditioning social factors or any other external considerations. Following the tradition of de Saussure, he makes a fundamental distinction between the general system (scheme) of a language (*la langue*; the code) and texts expressed by means of it (instances of *la parole*; otherwise called utterances or messages).[5] The objects of scientific analysis are concrete texts, but theory should make possible not only the description of these specific texts but also of all possible or conceivable ones which may (or may not) be realized in the future. On the basis of such analysis, Hjemslev says, "it should be possible to order these elements into classes according to their possibilities of combination. And it should be further possible to set up a general and exhaustive calculus of the possible combinations" (p. 9). But the language subjected to analysis is to be regarded as a closed system, self-contained and fully explainable in its own terms. The entities of linguistic form, Hjemslev assures us, are of an algebraic nature and have no natural designation; they can therefore be designated arbitrarily in many different ways (p. 105).

All this is very true, as far as it goes. The conventional and therefore in a sense arbitrary nature of linguistic expression has long since been recognized by specialists. Hjemslev's formulation of the thesis, though elaborate, is nothing new. His insistence on self-sufficient descriptions of languages as closed systems implies the synchronic point of view exclusively; signs of change are to be ignored as disturbing symptoms. Underlying this attitude there may be a quite unconscious fear that if psychology, anthropology and other social sciences are allowed to contribute to the under-

---

[5] L. Hjemslev, *Prolegomena to a Theory of Language*, transl. by F. T. Whitfield, second ed. (University of Wisconsin, 1961). The Danish original appeared in 1943.

standing of linguistic systems, then linguistic science will somehow lose its autonomy. The problem of interrelated disciplines exists in other fields as well. The physicist must take into account and make use of the findings of chemists, but he does not for that reason forfeit his status as representative of an independent science. The linguist may be expected to make use of pertinent findings from historical sociology (let us say) without jeopardy to his own independent status, provided only that he remembers to keep a clear distinction between the ancillary discipline and his own major concern: the study of linguistic systems as such.

Hjemslev's glossematic technique of description has been influential but has also evoked some sharp criticism. A very fundamental question was raised by P. L. Garvin in his review of the *Prolegomena*: namely how do we know that we have arrived at a complete knowledge of the "code" or linguistic system when we have confined ourselves to the analysis of a finite number of texts, presumably avoiding generalizations? (Or do we avoid them? Hjemslev's method of "empirical deduction" here looks suspiciously like induction.) A. Martinet has asked a similar question about the identification of *la langue* as seen by Hjemslev and those influenced by him. His critique included a warning against the dangers associated with the quest for unified "structures" in a language without due regard for exceptions and aberrations. This was in effect a warning against the dangers of over-simplification in any kind of structuralist approach, whether glossematic or other. The Soviet scholar O. S. Akhmanova published a detailed analysis of Hjemslev's theories in which she stressed, besides the objections already mentioned, the exclusion of meaning in the ordinary sense of the term: for Hjemslev's "purport" (Danish *mening*) is by no means the same thing.[6] She

---

[6] *Mening* or "purport" is defined as "a class of variables which manifest more than one chain under more than one syntagmatic, and/or more than one [paradigm under more than one paradigmatic." *Kæde* or "chain" is defined as a "class within a semiotic process" and *Semiotik* (semiotic) is "hierarchy, any of whose components admits of a further analysis into classes defined by mutual relation, so that any of these classes admits of an analysis into derivates defined by mutual mutation." See the very helpful list of defini-

protested not as much against the attempt to formulate a scheme for describing the general laws of language (общые законы языка —perhaps rendered better as the general patterns of dynamic linguistic relations?), as against the treatment of human language, an infinitely subtle and expansible system in all its forms, on the same level with elementary code substitutes such as the striking of clocks, the Morse alphabet and so on. There is indeed a qualitative difference involved here, which linguists are obliged to remember when they make use of the metaphor of a code in describing a *langue*. Some codes are expansible but others are not. Human speech belongs to the former category.

In his "deductive" method of analysis Hjemslev begins, as has been said, with concrete texts which are subdivided into units of diminishing length until one reaches what he calls formae or ultimate units. Similarly, American structuralists beginning with Bloomfield have practised a technique of dividing sentences into what they call Immediate Constituents (abbreviated as IC's; see ch. 6, sec. 4). Thus a normally complete sentence would first be split into a subject (with modifiers) and a predication (with complement and/or modifiers); each of these would then be further subdivided into word-groups forming minor constellations, as it were ("endocentric expressions" involving subordination) and so on down to the identification of the ultimate units (morphemes). The process is relatively easy in English, where linear order is more or less fixed and endocentric expressions are readily identified. But the grouping of IC's might well represent a more difficult problem in languages with a basically different structure, such as Eskimo.

Following out the possibilities suggested by subdivision into IC's, but departing from the method previously used, Zellig Harris has worked out a technique which he calls *String Analysis of Sentence Structure.*[7] English is chosen as the material for illustration. The term "string" is apparently chosen to emphasize

---

tions appended by Whitfield to his translation of *Omkring Sprogteoriens Grundlæggelse.* It is clear that semiotic is quite remote from semantics as discussed here in chapter 4.

[7] This is the title of the book by Harris (The Hague, 1962).

the linear nature of sentences: they are made up of units appearing in sequence, one after another. If we can identify a central unit or nucleus in a sentence, then we may speak of its adjuncts as appearing to the right or left of it, but there is no such relation as temporal simultaneity (such as might seem to be implied in the grammatical term subordination). Adjuncts moreover are not always contiguous to other parts of the constituent to which they belong, and a series of divisions into IC's will not indicate the relationship. Harris undertakes to present a system of analysis and notation which will permit of a concise generalized description of all possible types of English sentences.

Briefly speaking, he arrives at the identification of the elementary part S_0 of a sentence S by a series of cuttings or excisions in such a way that each time the residue is still recognizable as a complete sentence in the language. For instance, the English sentence "Today, automatic trucks from the factory which we just visited carry coal up the sharp incline" is subjected to a progression of excisions (first "Today," then "automatic," then "from the factory which we just visited," finally "up the sharp incline") until the residue "trucks carry coal" is isolated as S_0. The problem then arises: how describe in general terms the basic elements within such an S_0, as well as the elements attached to it in linear sequence, whether preceding it, incorporated within it, or following it?

As solution, Harris offers a quasi-algebraic set of formulas. The uninitiated reader should not be terrified by their esoteric appearance. Most of them are readily translatable into terms familiar to most of us, though sometimes the definitions offered vary from those to which we are accustomed. For instance the author gives us the following formula for a centre or nuclear string: $c_1 = \Sigma_i t V_{ij} \Omega_j$ —which represents the major type of English declarative sentence. Translated, this means that the first type (c_1) of centre string takes the form of (that is the meaning here of the $=$ sign) a sequence consisting of Σ_i (a given subject) followed by t representing some sort of tense-word or morpheme indicating tense, attached to a V or verb and followed by Ω which Harris calls "object" in his definitions. (Actually Ω might better be defined as completion: i.e., that which completes the verb, whether object, complement or attribute in conventional terminology.) The subscript i's and j's merely represent mutual relationships: V_{ij} stands for that subcategory of V (verb) which occurs with both Σ_i and Ω_j. In this way Harris elaborates a set of formulas intended to cover all—or almost all—types of English sentences. The elementary type of an English imperative centre string—for instance "Go home!"—is portrayed as c_3 = zero morphemic form of *you* [that is the absence of the word *you*] $+V_{ij}\Omega_j$! A negative centre string for instance "I did not come," is portrayed as $c_4 = \Sigma_i t$ *not* V_{ij}. (Here it is difficult to see what the subscript j refers to; there is no element following V.)

Harris himself has admitted (p. 25) that some types of English sentences can not be brought directly within the confines of string analysis, for instance in cases of reported discourse such as "I said that the control is certain." The formula for this type is given as NV' [*that*]... (where N stands for noun, V' stands for a special class of verbs such as *say, claim, report*, etc., and the brackets around *that* mean that it may or may not be present). Here the residue after string analysis is neither an independent sentence nor an adjunct of one. Special provision must be made for it. Yet the algebraic looking formulas worked out by Harris aim to offer a kind of short-hand statement of all the types of sentence which are acceptable in English. Reference to the formulas by "string-recognition process" would presumably enable one to report for each sentence whether it is well-formed or not; and if not, to establish what is lacking. Categorizing and testing by string-analysis and string-recognition may be expected to contribute towards the development of machine translation. The formalized technique would then offer a check on the results of such translation. To what extent all this will be realized in the realm of practical affairs, remains to be seen.

Before Harris, Chomsky had presented a different approach to the analysis of syntactic structures.[8] According to him, the aim of

---

[8] Noam Chomsky, *Syntactic Structures* (The Hague, 1957).

syntax is to construct a grammar which will be a guide for the production of sentences in a given language *L* but no non-sentences (that is, sequences unacceptable as such within the code of *L*). The operation of producing sentences is compared explicitly to the functioning of a machine which switches from one internal finite state to another as it produces one symbol (e.g. an English word) after another. "Each such machine," says Chomsky, "thus defines a certain language; namely, the set of sentences that can be produced in this way. Any language that can be produced by a machine of this sort we call a *finite state language*; and we can call the machine itself a *finite state grammar*" (p. 19). Taking as point of departure the subdivision of sentences into IC's, and assuming, as others have done, that the basic dichotomy is the division between *NP* (nominal phrase) and *VP* (verbal phrase), Chomsky suggests a series of operations, always passing from larger to smaller divisions and from more abstract to more concrete formulations, by which a sentence pattern may be described and an individual sentence may be "generated." In the elementary example given (p. 26) the arrow means the instruction "Rewrite as." Additional symbols are: *T* for the word-class known as the article, *N* for noun, *V* for verbal construction, + "followed by." The analysis proceeds as follows:

$$Sentence \rightarrow NP + VP$$
$$NP \rightarrow T + N$$
$$VP \rightarrow Verb + NP$$

giving finally: $T + N + Verb + T + N$.

This is the abstract representation of all sentences of the type "The man hit the ball." The steps in the analytic procedure are thus graphically represented:

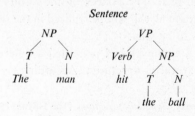

More elaborate abbreviations (symbols) must obviously be used to represent special categories. Thus *Verb* may be made up of *Aux* + *V* (an auxiliary followed by main verb); abbreviations are also needed to indicate the role played by inflexional morphemes (e.g. *V* + *S* would mean the specific form of a main verb when followed by the morpheme—including all its allomorphs—for a third person singular inflexion). In a scheme such as the one given above, *N* stands for all nouns without regard for their semantic classification such as we find in a thesaurus, and *Verb* (whether simple *V* or *Aux* + *V*) stands for all verbs of the type of *hit* (traditionally called transitive).

Now it happens that in the sentence here analyzed, one could interchange the two *N*'s and obtain a sentence that is still acceptable not only formally but semantically, namely "The ball hit the man." Balls do hit men. But it would not be possible to interchange the two *N*'s in "The man plucked the flower" and obtain a normally acceptable sentence. The same is true of sentences like "The man ate the duck" or "The man hated the tree." Men are not, in the world of practical experience, plucked by flowers or eaten by ducks or hated by trees. Yet in certain very special texts, such as modern poetry or popular folk tales, one might find such statements as "The flower plucked the man" or "The duck ate the man" or "The tree hated the man."

All of this simply means that context and semantic categories would have to be taken into account if the sentence "generated" from a given formula were to be acceptable in more than a formal sense. This observation is of course nothing new. The logical positivists pointed out long ago that a configuration of linguistic forms which is acceptable from the formal point of view may be entirely lacking in meaning from the practical point of view. This also means that a quality of words in sequence which has been called their collocability within contexts needs to be taken into account in "generating" sentences. Thus "A flaming wastepaper basket snored violently" might be eligible in a fairy tale, while "Twenty because tomorrow the had a it" would never be eligible.

And within the range of eligible collocations there are degrees of tolerance which need to be investigated.[9]

Within the framework of his $[\Sigma, F]$ grammar (which simply means a grammar based on a finite set Σ of initial strings of discourse and a finite set F of instructions of the type $X \rightarrow Y$), Chomsky works out an elaborate scheme of substitutions which may again be interpreted metaphorically as instructions to a machine. In the analysis of such a sentence, for instance, as "The man has been reading the book," suppose we have reached this stage (see p. 39):

$$\text{the} + \text{man} + \text{Verb} + \text{the} + \text{book.}$$

By instructions or rules for rewriting we obtain consecutively:

(1) *the* + *man* + *Aux* + *V* + *the* + *book*

(2) *the* + *man* + *S* + *have* + *en* + *be* + *ing* + *read* + *the* + *book*

(3) *the* + *man* + *have* + *S*#*be* + *en*#*read* + *ing*#*the* + *book*

(4) # *the* # *man* # *have* + *S* # *be* + *en* # *read* + *ing* # *the* # *book* #

The sign # is introduced to indicate divisions between words as they become clearly defined. A sequence like *have* + *S* means the main verb *have* as modified by affixing the morpheme ending for the third person singular, hence producing the word *has* (which is of course not the same as *have* with an added -*s*). Similarly *be* + *en* means the verb *be* as modified by affixing the morpheme ending for the perfect participle; but *have* + *en* would symbolically mean *had*, not *haven*.—It is by the application of morphophonemic rules that we derive from (4) and its predecessors the complete English sentence mentioned.

The very terminology of Chomsky's schematic description indicates that it too, like that of Harris, may serve the purposes of

---

[9] The important concept of linguistic collocability has been developed by Angus McIntosh, "Patterns and Ranges," *Language*, XXXVII (1961), 325–27. It has obvious importance for semantics. Dictionary synonyms, for instance, are not always collocable with the same following words. We may speak of an old man or an aged man or an old house—but not normally of an aged house. We also speak of Alexander the Great—but not Alexander the Big.

machine translation, though in a different way. Every time we press a button to obtain electric light we are giving "instructions" to an electronic system. In the same way we may "instruct" a machine to break down a sentence in any language and to transform it into a sentence of another. But this second demand is naturally far more exacting than the first. One might say, on a qualitatively higher level.

Linguists themselves have pointed out that there is a hierarchy of texts according to their adaptability to machine translations. The easiest would be—paradoxically, it might seem—those devoted to the exposition of the most exact and most abstract sciences. The reason is that here the phraseology is most conventional, the syntax least subject to innovation. At the other extreme would be free imaginative texts (poetry, fairy tales) where unexpected juxtapositions are frequent. Whether these latter are ever to be reduced to schematic formulation is a question. Human imagination has a way of evading established formulas. But in the meantime mechanical aids to human intercommunication on the scientific level must surely be welcomed. It is difficult to understand those linguists who express alarm over the advance of technology in this sphere. The only question which concerns all of us is: whether the newer techniques are to be used for the advancement of human welfare or the opposite.[10]

---

[10] To what extent Chomsky's generative grammar may be useful in the teaching of languages also remains to be seen. An attempt to use its technique in the analysis of a text of early Modern English has been made by Morton, W. Bloomfield and Leonard Newmark, *A Linguistic Introduction to the History of English* (New York, 1963), pp. 237 ff. The transformations worked out may possibly be appropriate for a machine, but a living student might well find them baffling.

CHAPTER 8

CONCLUSION

During the previous discussion, a number of problems of a general character have been touched upon. It will be appropriate to end with a summary statement about some of them.

One basic problem is the relation of linguistics to other sciences (see ch. 7, sec. 3). This has appeared with especial clarity in the investigation of previously unrecorded languages. Here it has been necessary to deal with phenomena on an exclusively synchronic basis. An investigator of unknown native languages in the Americas, Asia or Africa must rely on materials given by native informants and he must therefore inductively establish the entire linguistic structure. It is no wonder if he adopts a strictly synchronic point of view: he is in fact obliged to do so. Even when the present structure of the language points to a previous state he is not particularly interested in making the reconstructions thus suggested. He concentrates on describing the present code.

The demands and difficulties of such a task are obvious and the achievements have been impressive. A pioneer work of this sort was the study by the Russian scholar Otto Böhtlingk of the language of the Yakut people in Siberia (published 1851). Siberia and the Caucasus area have since been made the subject of many special investigations. In North America, Franz Boas initiated and inspired a whole series of studies of native Indian languages. They are being continued to this day, and the area has been extended to include Central and South America.

Now it is an interesting fact that much of the research on Indian languages has been carried out by specialists who were not primarily linguists, at least in the 19th-century sense of the term, but anthropologists. As such, they desired to obtain an all-inclusive picture of each culture concerned, its traditions, customs, social organization and so on. Language offered a most important means to the realization of their purpose. Their situation led to two contrasting tendencies. On the one hand, the technique of dealing with unknown languages lacking any written records led some investigators to regard them as systems in isolation, self-contained and self-explanatory. On the other hand, the use of such languages for purposes of sociological study inevitably raised the question: How, if at all, is the structure of a language related to its speakers' patterns of social behaviour and even their patterns of thought?

The problem here posed is not by any means a new one; it was raised by Wilhelm von Humboldt (died 1835) early in the 19th century and has been discussed by other European scholars in more recent times. A fresh impetus to the discussion was given by the American linguist-anthropologists Edward Sapir and Benjamin Lee Whorf. They formulated the basic question: to what extent is language a guide to social reality, and to what extent does it impose limitations on the thought processes of its users? What has been called the Sapir-Whorf hypothesis is the thesis that language functions, not only as a device for reporting experience, but as a way of defining experience for its speakers. In other words, it will determine—at least in certain categories—how they view the natural world, the universe, and their relations to one another within the speech community.

The hypothesis has been vigorously discussed, and some of the illustrations cited are interesting indeed. Relations of time and space are as a matter of fact handled quite differently in different languages. It has been pointed out that in the language of the Navaho Indians there is a strikingly pervasive concern with relations of motion in very manifold nuances. There are for instance no less than twelve verbal bases to express "he picks up something"; motion is involved in equivalents for static English expressions as "to make plans" (literally in Navaho: "move happenings about here and there") or "to be busy" (literally: "one moves continuously about with reference to it") or even the noun meaning moon ("a hoop-like object has rolled out").[1] One might say that for the Navaho even more than for the Greek philosopher Heraclitus, all things are in a state of flux. It has been pointed out, again, that Navaho has but one term to designate the colours blue and green together: does it mean that the speakers see no differences in the colour spectrum at this point? Or in the social sphere, some languages include a far more elaborate nomenclature for family relationship than others (in English a nephew is a nephew, but in Polish you have to know whether he is a sister's or a brother's son before you can call him *siostrzeniec* or *bratanek*). Finally, there are languages which, according to report, do not possess the category which we should call the generalized common noun, for instance snow-in-general, parrots-in-general, etc. For the Eskimo, every reference to snow must apparently indicate its precise nature (hard or soft, etc.); for the Bororo of Brazil there are said to be many names for individual species of parrots, but no inclusive term for all parrots. Does this mean, therefore, that speakers of such languages are to be eternally incapable of studying the philosophy of Plato or Kant, which require such generalized conceptions as the eternal, unchanging idea of a parrot-in-general (apart from all minor mutations)—or of the *Ding-an-sich*?

Certainly not. The distinguished predecessor of both Sapir and Whorf, Franz Boas emphasized long ago that human beings are quite capable of rising above the restriction of their linguistic systems when the need is pointed out to them. They will themselves deduce a general Platonic noun for snow or parrot with the aid of some patient and sympathetic questioning. And as Boas pointed out, they will often put to shame their interrogator by their acute awareness of differences in phenomena which he—confined within the Indo-European system of categories—had not noticed. These who look upon a linguistic system as a prepared strait-jacket for thought forget that human beings are quite capable of modifying it consciously, as for instance when a scientific vocabulary is

---

[1] H. Hoijer, "Cultural Implications of Some Navaho Linguistic Categories," *Language*, XXVII (1951), 111-20.

deliberately created for a special field of research. Elementary systems are potentially capable of being developed into more and more complex ones, as has been demonstrated in the case of "pidginized" languages or *linguae francae*.[2] Whether or not the potentialities are to be realized will depend on non-linguistic factors of social history.

These problems indicate areas in which the cooperation of linguists with psychologists, sociologists, and others in the social sciences may lead to valuable results.

Another problem of wider implications is that of the standardizing and unifying of a language. In those peoples possessing a literature (oral or written) and a literary tradition, there is often a noticeable discrepancy between the languages of literature and various forms of popular speech. In a class society the discrepancy will be an index of the separation of those possessing an accepted standard type of education (in the broadest sense) and those lacking it. The situation is further complicated by the existence of regional dialects within a national speech community, for these in turn may be quite widely diversified insofar as each one reflects various degrees of accessibility on the part of the speakers to a standard education.

When a standard speech is associated with class privileges, it may naturally be resented by the underprivileged. Yet the latter, in struggling for their rights and for the elimination of class distinction, desire most of all to participate in the sum total of the culture of their people: hence to master the richest expression of it in language, not an impoverished one. Thus the problem of a unified speech within nations will be solved, not by rules and regulations imposed from above, but by making accessible to all the maximum

---

[2] Robert A. Hall, Jr., in *Hands off Pidgin English* (Sydney, 1955), makes the interesting point that a much-simplified, pidginized form of Malay, developed by the Dutch for linguistic intercourse with their Indonesian subjects and popularly known as Bazaar Malay, became a vehicle of the movement of independence and later the national language of the Republic. A *lingua franca* may perform a valuable service as a means of communication among scattered groups speaking widely different languages.

education they are capable of absorbing, in a milieu purged of special economic privilege.

On a world scale the problem of unity versus diversity also exists. It is recognized that linguistic differences among peoples and nations have placed barriers between them. For this reason various attempts have been made to propagate an international language, artificially constructed. Well-known is Esperanto, an early effort in this direction made by Zamenhof (a Polish physician, died 1917). Yet Esperanto was after all a provincial creation, assuming that its learners were already acquainted with the elements of Western European languages, especially those descended from Latin. True enough, Latin and also Greek elements have been made widely familiar through the more or less international (Western) terminology of modern sciences. But what of the languages of Asia and Africa which have their own terminology? To be truly international on a global scale such a created language should be equally easy to master by a speaker of Tagalog in Southern India, Haussa in Africa, and Navaho in North America—not to speak of Japanese and various forms of Chinese. A truly international language constructed with this end in view might be far more difficult to learn—at least for many people—than any one of the existing natural languages, for instance English or Mandarin Chinese or Hindu. All have a relatively clear structure, and being human, all three are capable of infinite expansion to express human needs.

Let us suppose that some international language (whether natural or artificial) were accepted on a world scale. Would it long remain unified, or would it in turn break down into local dialects again giving rise to separate languages mutually unintelligible? This is a rather theoretical question at the present time. So far in human history we have witnessed diversification in the forms of human speech: Indo-European was divided into many groups; of these Germanic was subdivided into subgroups; among these the Scandinavian today exhibits separate languages as divergent as Icelandic and Norwegian, while each of them contains within itself internal differentiations. Yet we may even now consider the factors tending in the opposite direction. Modern techniques of communication have already advanced to the point where the promulgation of unified standards has become enormously facilitated by films, radio and television. Here it is not so much a matter of deliberate instruction as influential example. The receiver unconsciously imitates what he has heard. It may well be that we are on the verge of a new era in which previously unheard-of techniques facilitating communication will be developed. Whether they will lead to linguistic unification of the human race remains to be seen. It may be pointed out that one contemporary technique—namely instantaneous translations transmitted through earphones at multilingual conferences—has actually reduced the need for a single international language.

One thing alone is certain: in language as in all other human affairs, the only permanence is change. As for the direction of change, that depends on the interplay of many factors, both internal and external. In all of these, men's directed social effort is of primary importance.

SUPPLEMENTARY BIBLIOGRAPHICAL NOTES

CHAPTER 1

On the development of classical grammar see R. H. Robins, *Ancient and Mediaeval Grammatical Theory in Europe with Particular Reference to Modern Linguistic Doctrine* (London, 1951); also Otto Jespersen, *Language: Its Nature, Development and Origin* (London, 1922). The authoritative general survey of linguistic science to 1900 is Holger Pedersen's *Linguistic Science in the Nineteenth Century*, tr. John Webster Spargo (Harvard University Press, 1931, reprinted as *The Discovery of Language* by Indiana University Press, 1959). The full title of Rasmus Rask's pioneer study on early Scandinavian in relation to other Germanic languages was *Undersøgelse om det gamle nordiske eller islandske Sprogs Oprindelse* (Copenhagen, 1818).

The example of dialect distribution of words for *mouse* and *house* in Netherlands territory is taken from Leonard Bloomfield, *Language* (New York, 1933), pp. 328 f. This is a book which will be frequently referred to in ensuing chapters. For early speculations on the origin of language see Herder's *Abhandlung über den Ursprung der Sprache* as edited by Th. Matthias (Leipzig, 1901) and Ludwig Noiré, *Der Ursprung der Sprache* (Mainz, 1877).

CHAPTER 2

Much of this chapter is based on the monumental work edited by Antoine Meillet and Marcel Cohen, *Les Langues du monde* (2nd ed., Paris, 1952), to which grateful acknowledgement is herewith made. Details have been added from special studies which will be mentioned later. Some general books on linguistics include concise surveys of the world's linguistic families, e.g. Louis H. Gray, *Foundations of Language* (New York, 1939), chs. 11 and 12, and Winfred P. Lehmann, *Historical Linguistics* (New York, 1962), ch. 2. Father W. Schmidt's *Sprachfamilien und Sprachenkreise der Erde* (Heidelberg, 1926) is rich in materials, but some of the genetic groupings proposed by the author are highly speculative.

CHAPTER 3

The example of infixed Welsh pronouns is taken from John Strachan, *An Introduction to Early Welsh* (Manchester University Press, 1937). The terminology of morphemic analysis was made familiar by Bloomfield in his *Language* (1933); it has been since applied and amplified by specialists such as Eugene Nida in *Morphology: The Descriptive Analysis of Words* (University of Michigan, 1949) and Zellig Harris in *Methods in Structural Linguistics* (University of Chicago, 1951). On the philosophical questions involved in the problem of meaning as related to morphemes, see also the notes to ch. 4. The desirability of referring to extralinguistic factors as a short-cut to meaning was pointed out by Einar Haugen, "Directions in Modern Linguistics," *Language*, XXVII (1951), 211–22.

CHAPTER 4

F. de Saussure's exposition of signifiers and things signified is to be found in his *Cours de linguistique générale* (Paris, 1913), pp. 97 ff. The very influential book by C. K. Ogden and I. A. Richards on the same problem is *The Meaning of Meaning* (London, 1936). For an elaboration of Bloomfield's doctrine of meaning see Eugene Nida, "A System for the Description of Semantic Elements," *Word*, VII (1951), 1–14. M. Bréal's book was translated as *Semantics* (London, 1900), now recently reprinted (New York, 1964). The theory of semantic fields was propounded by J. Trier in *Der deutsche Wortschatz im Sinnbezirk des Verstandes* (Heidelberg, 1931); see Suzanne Öhmann, "Theories of the Linguistic Field," *Word*, IX (1953), 123–34 and also W. Rothwell's critique in *Modern Language Review*, LVII (1962), 25–30.

Studies on the subject of language and thought by psychologists (too little known by linguists, it may be said) are very numerous. A useful introduction is offered in the booklet of that title by John B. Carroll (London: Prentice-Hall, 1964). Still interesting is *Мышление и Речь* by L. S. Vygotski (Moscow-Leningrad, 1934), now available in English as *Thought and Language*, tr. E. Hanfmann and G. Vakar (Cambridge, Mass.: MIT Press, 1962).

Two recommended general studies on semantics are those by Stephen Ullmann, *The Principles of Semantics*, 2nd ed. (Glasgow, 1957) and his later *Semantics* (London and New York, 1962). A critical review of various schools is given by the Russian scholar Vladimir Zvegintsev in his *Semasiologia* (Moscow University, 1957), available in Polish as *Semazjologia*, tr. J. Fleszner (Warsaw, 1962).

CHAPTER 5

On the transition from picture to alphabets, see Hans Jensen, *Geschichte der Schrift* (Hannover, 1925); also I. J. Gelb, *A Study of Writing* (2nd ed., University of Chicago, 1963). The examples from ancient Egyptian are taken from Alan Gardiner, *Egyptian Grammar* (2nd ed., Oxford, 1950). The remarks on Chinese classifiers are based on K. B. J. Karlgren, *Sound and Symbol in Chinese* (rev. ed., Oxford, 1962). The article "Alphabet" in the *Encyclopaedia Britannica* illustrates the relation of Sinaiatic, Semitic and Greek writing. On the development of Cyrillic see В. А. Устрин, *1100 Лет Славянской Азбуки* (Moscow, 1963). The basis of the IPA is explained in *The Principles of the International Phonetic Association* (1912).

A recent account of historical sound changes and sound relationships is given by Winfred P. Lehmann as cited above in the notes to ch. 2. For Indo-European specifically see A. Meillet, *Introduction à l'étude comparative des langues indo-européennes* (7th ed., Paris, 1934). On the question of Hittite sounds see Edgar H. Sturtevant, *The Indo-Hittite Laryngeals* (Baltimore, 1942); on ancient Cretan, John Chadwick, *The Decipherment of Linear B* (Cambridge, 1960). The relation of individual lapses to general sound changes has been discussed by E. H. Sturtevant, *An Introduction to Linguistic Science* (Yale University, 1947), ch. 9. Edward Sapir proposed the term drift in his *Language* (New York, 1922).

CHAPTER 6

The dictionary of linguistic terminology offered by J. Marouzeau, *Lexique de la terminologie linguistique* (Paris, 1951), is still useful for the clarification of such expressions as *discours, parties de* (i.e. parts of speech), but it should now be supplemented by Mario, A. Pei, *A Glossary of Linguistic Terminology* (Columbia University, 1966). John Ries, *Was ist Syntax?* (Marburg, 1894; 2nd ed., Prague, 1927) remains stimulating to this day.

All statements about the Mende language are based on the study by Ethel G. Aginsky as cited in n. 15. Material concerning Ewe is derived from Diedrich Westermann, *A Study of the Ewe Language* (Oxford, 1930). For Japanese see G. B. Sansom, *An Historical Grammar of Japanese* (Oxford, 1928). Illustrations from the Bantu languages come from Sir Harry Johnson, *A Comparative Study of the Bantu and Semi-Bantu Languages*, 2 vols. (Oxford, 1919–22).

The interrelation of stylistics and linguistics has been discussed from several points of view in a collection of essays, *Style in Language*, ed. Thomas A. Sebeok (New York, 1960). The distinction between casual and non-casual utterances is here made by C. F. Voegelin, pp. 57–68. Soviet scholars have provided valuable guides to stylistic analysis. See as but one example E. Riesel, *Abriss der deutschen Stilistik* (Moscow, 1954). Descriptive grammars occasionally include a consideration of style, e.g. T. Grzebieniowski, *Morfologia i składnia języka angielskiego* (Warsaw, 1964)—a textbook of English designed for Polish students. This combination of interests is surely to be welcomed.

CHAPTER 7

A readable introduction to the origins and nature of probability theory is provided by Horace C. Levinson, *Chance, Luck and Statistics* (New York, 1963). See further George A. Miller, *Language and Communication* (New York, 1951) for statistical methods applied to language. The two major works of George Kingsley Zipf in this field were: *Selected Studies of Relative Frequency in Language* (Harvard University, 1932) and *The Psycho-Biology of Language* (Boston, 1935). Later developments are represented by G. Udny Yule, *The*

Statistical Study of Literary Vocabulary (Cambridge, 1944) and G. Herdan, *Language as Choice and Chance* (Amsterdam, 1956).

Colin Cherry, *On Human Communication* (New York, 1957) offers a good introduction to the theory of communication; here information as negative entropy is discussed pp. 214 ff. The psychological behaviourism of the Bloomfield school has been much discussed. For a critical estimate see for instance Klaus Hanssen, "Wege und Ziele des Strukturalismus," *Zeitschrift für Anglistik und Amerikanistik*, VI (1958), 341–81; on the other side C. C. Fries, "The Bloomfield 'School'," *Trends in European and American Linguistics*, ed. Christine Mohrman, Alf Sommerfelt, Joshua Whatmough (Utrecht, 1963). The general position of social behaviourism is presented by Charles Morris in *Signs, Language and Behavior* (New York, 1946). A short documented discussion of glossematics is given by Henning Spang-Hansen in *Trends*, just referred to, pp. 128–64. Garvin's review of the *Prolegomena* by Hjemslev appeared in *Language*, XXX (1954), 69–95; Martinet expressed his doubts in a review of a book by K. Togeby, *Word*, IX (1953), 78–82; O. S. Akhmatova devoted a critical article to glossematics in *Вопросы Языкознания* (1953, na 3), 25–47.

For those who wish to read further in contemporary linguistics, the following will be useful. First of all, Simeon Potter, *Language in the Modern World* (Penguin Books, 1960), as supplement to the present sketch. On a more, advanced level: Charles F. Hockett, *A Course in Modern Linguistics* (New York, 1958); A. A. Hill, *Introduction to Linguistic Structures* (New York, 1958); H. A. Gleason, Jr., *An Introduction to Descriptive Linguistics*, rev. ed. (New York, 1961); Robert A. Hall, Jr., *Introductory Linguistics* (Philadelphia and New York, 1964).

INDEX OF TERMS DEFINED

acteme 150
adjective 120
adjuncts of sentences 154
adverb 120
agglutination 29f.
agglutinating languages 44
agreement 130
analytic languages 44
allomorph 52f.
alphabet 88
aspect 121
assimilation 107
— complete 108
— partial 108
— progressive 109
— regressive 109
— of vowels 108

behavioureme 150
behaviourism, linguistic 63
— social 63, 149
binit, bit 145
bound forms 45ff., 69

case 6, 51
casual discourse 134
Centum languages 24
classifier 90
code 144
communication theory 145
complementary distribution 96
conditioned variant 96
congruence 130
conjunction 123
collocations 158
connotation 75f.
consciousness, postulate of 65
consonant, fricative 94
— nasal 95
— plosive 94
— spirant 94

— stop 94
— vocalic 100
— voiced 94
— voiceless 94
continuum, linguistic 99

denotation 75f.
description "etic" 149
— "emic" 149
determinant 90
diachronic description 57f.
dialect 21
diphthong 99
dissimilation 110
drift, linguistic 105

ellipsis 81
"emic" 149, 150
endocentric construction 131
entropy, negative 147
episememe 71
ethnosememe 71n.
— "etic" 149
etymology 57
exocentric construction 131

families of languages 22
finite state grammar 156
formae 153
frame sentences 60
free forms 45ff., 50, 69
free variant 98
function words 123
functional yield 98
fused forms 56

gender 120
glossematics 150
government, syntactic 130
Grimm's law 12

homonym 78

idealism, linguistic 63
ideogram 88
immediate constituent 116
individual lapses 111
infix 48
inflectional languages 44
inflexion 29f., 51
information 145
international language 164
International Phonetic Association 93
International Phonetic Alphabet 94
isolating languages 44

jargon 84
juncture 61, 101
— closed 101
— open 101
— terminal 101

kineme 150

macrosememe 71
Markoff chain 144
meaning 64, 68
— abstraction of 82
— extension of 81
— restriction of 81
— transfer of 82
metaphor 82
metathesis 111
minimal pairs 98
monogenesis 43
morph 52
morpheme 53, 62
morphemes, homonymous 53f.
— productive 55
— unproductive 55
morphology 51

national languages 21
Neo-grammarians 15
neologism 55

noise 144
noncasual discourse 134
noun 120

order of sentence elements 129

palatalization 107
parts of speech 117
phoneme 96
phonemic transcription 96
phonetic transcription 93
picture writing 87
pidgin languages 163
polygenesis 43
popular etymology 55
predicate 118f.
prefix 48
preposition 120, 123
probability 138
— transitional 144, 147

rebus writing 90
reconstructed forms 106
redundancy 147
reference 70
referent 70
rhetoric 9
root 49f.

Sapir-Whorf hypothesis 161
satem languages 24
secret languages 84
semantics 68
semantics, general 77
semantic change 74
— — meliorative 79f.
— — pejorative 80
semantic field 72
seme 71
sememe 70
sentence 113, 115
sign 67f.
Signifiant 68f.
Signifié 68f.
sound change 102
— — "unconditioned" 104f.

spectrograph 102
string analysis of sentences 153
structuralism 70
style 133
stylistics 135
subject 118f.
substratum 43
subordination 131
suffix 48
superstratum 43
syllable 99f.
syllabic nuclei 100
syllabic writing 89
symbol 67f., 70
symmetry of phonemes 103
synchronic description 56, 58
syntax 128
synthetic languages 44

tabu 84
tagmeme 127

taxeme 127n.
tense 121

umlaut 108
uttereme 150

verb 120
verbal noun 121
vowel 99
— rounded 95
— unrounded 95
— harmony 29, 34, 60

word 60f.

zero suffix 51

INDEX OF NAMES[1]

Aelfric 9
Aginsky, E. A., 169
Akhmanova, O. S., 152, 170
Albanian 16, 28
Algonquin-Wakash languages 41
Altaic languages 33
Amerindian languages 40
Andres de Olmos 125
Arawak languages 42
Aristotle 6
Armenian languages 16, 28
Australian languages 38

Bacon, Roger 8
Baltic languages 24
Bantu languages 39
Basque 30
Bede 9
Bloomfield, L., 70, 153, 167
Bloomfield, M. W., 159
Boas, F., 41, 160, 162
Bohtlingk, O., 160
Bopp, F., 11
Bréal, M., 71, 168
Brugmann, K., 15
Burmese 36

Carib languages 42
Carnap, R., 151
Carroll, J. B., 168
Caucasian languages 38
Celtic languages 16, 48
Cicero 7
Chadwick, J., 169
Chaucer, G., 8, 78, 143
Cherry, C. C., 145n., 148, 170
Chinese 35
Chomsky, N., 155, 155n., 156, 158

Cohen, Marcel, 167
Curtius, G., 13

Donatus 7
Dravidian languages 38

Eaton, Helen, 140, 141n.
Edda, poetic 10
Erasmus 9
Eskimo-Aleutian languages 41

Fick, A., 13
Finno-Ugric languages 28ff.
Fleszner, J., 168
Fries, C.C., 122n., 170

Gardiner, A., 168
Garvin, H. L., 152, 170
Gelb, I. J., 168
Germanic languages 16, 26
Gerson, J., 143
Gesner, K., 9
Gleason, H. A. Jr., 170
Gray, L. H., 167
Greenberg, J., 71
Grimm, J., 12
Grosseteste, Robert 9
Grzebieniowski, T., 169

Hall, R. A., Jr., 163n., 170
Halle, M., 145n.
Hamitic languages 32, 38

[1] Individual languages are not indexed, but only linguistic families and groups.

Harris, Z., 153, 153n., 154f., 158, 167
Haufmann, E., 168
Haugen, E., 168
Hansen, K., 170
Hellenic languages 16, 25
Herdan, G., 143
Herder, G., 17, 167
Hill, A. A., 170
Hittite 16, 28
Hjemslev, L., 150, 151n., 153, 170
Hockett, C. F., 170
Hoijer, H., 71n., 162n.
Hoka-Siou languages 41
Humboldt, W. von, 161

Indo-European languages 11, 16, 23, 164
Indo-Iranian languages 16, 17, 23
Isidore of Seville 7
Italic languages 16, 25

Jacobus de Voragine 8
Jakobson, R., 145n.
Japanese 37
Jensen, H., 168
Jespersen, O., 167
Johnson, Sir Harry, 168
Johnson, S., 10
Jones, Sir William 11

Kaeding, F. W., 141n.
Kant, E., 162
Karlgren, K. B. J., 168
Keynes, M., 75
Khoin languages 39
Kichua 42
Korean 36
Korzybski, A., 77

Lactantius 7
Lehmann, W. P., 167f.
Levinson, H. C., 169

Malay-Polynesian languages 37, 40
Markoff, A. A., 144
Marouzeau, J., 169

Martinet, A., 152
Matthias, Th., 167
Maya-Soke languages 42
McIntosh, A., 158n.
McQuown, A. N., 119n.
Meillet, A., 106, 167, 169
Miller, G. A. 169
Mohrman, C., 170
Mongol languages 34
Morris, C., 170

Na-Dene languages 41
Newmark, L., 159
Nida, E., 70, 167, 168
Noiré, L., 167

Ogden, C. K., 168
Öhmann, S., 168

Paleo-Siberian languages 34
Pāṇini 5
Paul, H., 118n.
Pedersen, H., 167
Pei, M. A., 169
Penutia languages 41
Pike, K., 149, 149n.
Pittman, R. S., 126n.
Plato, 6, 162
Poe, E. A., 142
Porzig, W., 63
Pott, A., 13
Potter, S., 170
Priscian 7
Pushkin, A., 145n.

Rabanus Maurus 8
Rask, R., 11, 167
Romance languages 26, 43
Ries, J., 169
Riesel, E., 169
Robins, R. H., 167
Rothwell, W., 168

Sapir, E., 41, 105, 118n., 162, 169
Sansom, G. B., 169
Saussure, F. de, 144, 151, 168

Schaff, A., 77n.
Schlegel, A. W. von, 11
Schlegel, F. von, 11
Schleicher, A. 13
Schmidt, Wilhelm 167
Sebeok, T. A., 169
Semitic languages 31, 38
Sino-Tibetan languages 35, 40
Skeat, W. W., 5
Slavic languages 24
Sommerfelt, A., 170
Spang-Hanssen, H., 170
Spargo, W., 167
Steinthal, H., 17
Strachan, J., 167
Sturtevant, E. H., 169
Sudanese-Guinean languages 39

Thomas à Kempis 143
Tibetan 36
Tocharian languages 16, 28
Togeby, K., 170
Trier, J., 72, 168
Tunguz languages 34
Turkic languages 33

Ullman, S., 168
Ural-Altaic languages 33, 40
Ustrin, V. A., 168
Uto-Aztec-Tono languages 41

Vakar, G., 168
Varro 7
Verner, Karl 13
Vygotsky, L. S., 168

Westermann, D., 169
Whatmough, J., 170
Whitfield, F. T., 151, 153n.
Whorf, B. L., 161f.

Yule, G. U., 143, 169

Zamenhof, L., 164
Zipf, G. K., 142, 169
Zvegintsev, V., 168